The Rules of Insanity

The Rules of Insanity

*Moral Responsibility and the
Mentally Ill Offender*

Carl Elliott

STATE UNIVERSITY
OF NEW YORK PRESS

Published by
State University of New York Press, Albany

For information, address the State University of New York Press,
State University Plaza, Albany, NY 12246

Production by Bernadine Dawes • Marketing by Fran Keneston

Library of Congress Cataloging-in-Publication Data

Elliott, Carl, 1961–
    The rules of insanity : moral responsibility and the mentally ill offender / Carl Elliott.
        p.   cm.
    Includes bibliographical references and index.
    ISBN 0-7914-2951-2 (hc : acid-free). — ISBN 0-7914-2952-0 (pb : alk. paper)
    1. Insanity — Jurisprudence.   2. Criminal liability.   I. Title.
    RA1151.E56   1996
    614'.1 — dc20   95-34254
                                                                              CIP

1 2 3 4 5 6 7 8 9 10

353136

For Scott Campbell

Contents

Acknowledgments

The most pleasant part of the generally disagreeable task of writing a book is acknowledging your intellectual debts. I have accumulated more debts than most writers, and to no one am I more indebted than to Robin Downie. This book began while I was a postgraduate in philosophy under his supervision at Glasgow University. It is only now that I am supervising students myself that I realize fully how far beyond the demands of duty he went, both as a mentor and as a friend. I am also particularly grateful to Elizabeth Telfer, who, like Robin, helped to shape the book with her thoughtful critical remarks.

This short book took a long time to write, and it was written at many different points on the globe. My wife Ina and I spent a wonderful year in Dunedin, New Zealand, where I was a postdoctoral fellow at the Bioethics Research Centre at the University of Otago. There I was fortunate to work closely with Grant Gillett, who taught me about psychopaths and Wittgenstein, and who went out of his way to help me in innumerable ways. I am also indebted to Paul Mullen, then Chair of Psychological Medicine at Otago, for allowing me to accompany him on psychiatric rounds at Cherry Farm Hospital, and for his contributions to the Philosophy and Psychiatry Seminar. Rick Howard of the Department of Psychological Medicine was also extremely helpful in discussing his work on psychopaths.

Part of the manuscript were also written and revised at the Center for Clinical Medical Ethics at the University of Chicago, where I was a fellow; at the East Carolina University Department of Medical Humanities, where I was a visiting professor; at the University of Natal Medical School in Durban, South Africa, where I was a research fellow; and at the McGill University Centre for Medicine, Ethics and Law. My thanks to all these institutions for their

research support. I am especially grateful to Al Mele, John Lantos, Mary Ma-
howald, Norval Morris, Rick Kodish, Richard Gunderman, and Loretta Kopel-
man for their comments on various chapters of the book. A shorter version of
chapter 3 appeared in the *Journal of Applied Philosophy* as "Moral Responsibility, Psychiatric Disorders and Duress" (1991; 8:1, 45–56).

This book would have been much harder to write if my two brothers, Britt
and Hal, had not been trained in philosophy and psychiatry, respectively. Much
of what appears in these pages emerged from conversations with them. Finally,
I owe more than I can express here to Scott Campbell, who first made me aware
of what philosophy is really about.

Introduction

Mentally ill people often do crazy things, and occasionally these things are unlawful, offensive, or morally wrong. Ordinarily, we do not blame a person for acting wrongly if he is mentally ill. The problem is that sane people do crazy things too. In fact, just what counts as craziness is often exactly the problem. How do we tell which people are mentally ill or disordered enough to be exonerated from blame for their actions, and which are sane and responsible?

This book attempts to give some answers to questions about the conditions under which mentally disordered people should be held morally responsible for their actions. The answer it gives is not simple. For example, judgments of responsibility depend on, among other things, what sort of mental disorder the person in question has. The inexhaustible array of mental disturbances that the mind is capable of displaying differ in morally important ways; addressing the question of responsibility means addressing the moral implications of these disturbances.

Wittgenstein is said to have stressed a difference between his philosophical aims and those of most other philosophers. While other philosophers tried to show that things that looked different were really the same, Wittgenstein said he wanted to show that things that looked the same were really different. For this reason he considered taking as a motto for his *Philosophical Investigations* a quotation from King Lear: "I'll teach you differences." This is an approach for which I have some sympathy. I am convinced there is no simple way to sum up in a single rule, or even a concise series of rules, when a mentally disordered person ought to be excused from moral responsibility for his actions. All mental disorders are not the same, especially not from a moral standpoint.

1

So I want to issue a warning. My efforts here have not been directed toward developing a "theory" of responsibility for the mentally disordered or a system of rules to explain which individuals ought to be exonerated from moral responsibility for their actions. This book is less about generalities than about particulars. One important message is that decisions about the accountability of any individual will depend on the particular circumstances of his case and the specific ways in which the disorder has affected his thinking. Legal tests of insanity have often tried to summarize in a few sentences just what sorts of mental impairment are relevant to criminal responsibility. While there are good reasons for the law to take such a simple approach, morality is more complicated.

Thus, the title of the book is ironic. Morally speaking, there are no rules of insanity. Still, there is some accuracy in the irony. I have not laid down the "rules of insanity," but I have approached the problem in a relatively systematic way. By placing different sorts of psychiatric disorder in various moral categories, I have tried to make the moral questions easier to understand.

Another aim of the book, then, has been taxonomic: an effort to impose some artificial order on a necessarily disordered subject. I have started by arguing that there is little that one can usefully say about the responsibility of mentally ill persons as a class. There are many mental illnesses, some of which, over time, will become more properly called neurological illnesses, others of which may be more properly called problems of living, and still others of which may never fit into either category. All of these have different implications for moral responsibility. So, to say anything useful about the responsibility of mentally ill people, it is necessary to say something about many different types of mental illness, as well as about the specific circumstances of individual cases.

Concepts and Taxonomy

A few words need to be said about the conceptual framework of the book, as well as the "moral taxonomy" of mental disorders that I have set out. In general, a mentally sound person can offer two types of excuse for her actions, ignorance and compulsion: "I didn't know what I was doing," or "I couldn't help doing it." Similarly, insanity pleas have generally focused on two types of test, "cognitive" and "volitional." Cognitive tests generally ask whether a person's mental illness prevented her from knowing what she was doing, and volitional tests ask whether her mental illness prevented her from being able to control what she was doing.[1]

Now, two broad categories of mental disorder can be divided up in roughly the same way. From a moral standpoint, some disorders are important because they affect a person's volitions or desires, while others are important because they affect a person's beliefs. Those that affect a person's desires (discussed in chapter 3) might include impulse-control disorders such as kleptomania, pyromania, and pathological gambling; the obsessive-compulsive disorder; and some psychosexual disorders such as exhibitionism, voyeurism, pedophilia, and some fetishes. The disorders that affect a person's beliefs and other cognitive abilities (discussed in chapter 6) would include psychoses such as schizophrenia, psychotic depression, and the bipolar affective disorder (or manic-depressive disorder).

These two categories of mental disorder, I will argue, can exonerate a person from moral responsibility for her actions in what are, from a conceptual standpoint, fairly straightforward ways — compulsion and ignorance. The devil is in the details, of course, and actual cases are never so simple. This point will become abundantly clear over the course of the book. But conceptually, these sorts of cases are relatively easy to understand. The disorders affect a person's responsibility because they affect her beliefs or her desires, making it the case that she did not know what she was doing, or that it was very hard for her to avoid doing it.

After this, however, there are some trouble spots. One of the most troubling is the area of "personality disorders" — relatively longstanding, maladaptive character traits that may affect a person's life dramatically, often making her miserable, perhaps more often making other people miserable. People with personality disorders are troubling because very often they come from backgrounds that argue for sympathy and understanding; on the other hand, they often behave very badly, and do it intentionally. Perhaps, as Philip Larkin said, "They fuck you up, your Mum and Dad"; but often this is something that we do a good job of on ourselves. We both make and are made by our characters. Seen in this way, the fairness of blaming a person with a personality disorder for his offenses is open for debate.

I argue in chapter 4 that, in general, we *ought* to hold people with personality disorders morally responsible for their actions. In that chapter, I argue that judgments of responsibility are judgments about the connection between an agent and an action, and that this connection is unaffected by a personality disorder. However, while this is the case in general, one exception stands out, and that is the psychopathic personality. The psychopath is the star of chapter 5. The reason the psychopath is exceptional lies in the particular, peculiar nature of his problems, which, it has been argued, include an inability to understand *moral concerns*. If a person cannot understand morality — that is, if he truly cannot understand that what he is doing is wrong — then it seems unfair to blame him when he acts wrongly. The psychopathic personality is the most intriguing disorder of all from a philosophical perspective, both because the psychopath's deficiencies are not exactly what one might expect and because they call into question some basic assumptions about what it is for a person to "understand" morality.

This leaves one final category for the book's moral taxonomy, those patients who are so severely disordered that they cannot be considered morally responsible agents. It has been said that whom the gods would destroy, they first make mad — but whom the gods would hold blameless, they must make very mad indeed. At least, this is the view of the American Psychiatric Association, which says that if an offender is to be exonerated from criminal responsibility on grounds of insanity, her disorder must be *serious,* somewhere close to the severity of the psychoses.[2] While from a moral standpoint there are problems with this rule, it does point to that class of *very* severely disordered patients, such as those with chronic schizophrenia, whose incapacities place them outside our scheme of moral responsibility altogether. In chapter 7, I suggest that without a certain minimal level of mental ability, an individual cannot be considered a morally responsible agent, and thus cannot be considered responsible for her actions.

To summarize: from a moral standpoint, at least five categories of mental disorders are especially important for responsibility: disorders of volition, disorders affecting beliefs, the personality disorders, the psychopathic personality, and those very severe disorders of various types which place a person outside our scheme of responsibility altogether. These categories overlap quite a bit, and from a psychiatric standpoint, they jumble together disorders that might otherwise have nothing to do with each other. Nonetheless, they are a useful way of conceptualizing the disorders that are particularly relevant to questions of responsibility.

Chronology

The chronology of the book follows a slightly different path. The reason for this is that in order to understand judgments of the moral responsibility of persons with mental illnesses, it is necessary to understand the basic vocabulary and concepts underlying those judgments in the mentally sound. It is also helpful to have some idea of how the law has dealt with mentally ill offenders. For this reason, the book begins not with specific disorders but with two chapters on the groundwork of assessing responsibility. Chapter 1 deals with insanity pleas: the ways that the law has dealt with mentally disordered persons in the past, the wrong turns that the law has taken, and relevance of these wrong turns to the main focus of the book, moral responsibility. Chapter 2 lays out the general approach to questions of moral responsibility that underlies the rest of the book. That approach is relatively straightforward, and it is similar to the one that Aristotle set out in Book III of the *Nicomachean Ethics:* a person should not be excused from responsibility unless he has acted unknowingly or unwillingly. In ordinary judgments of responsibility, most excuses are variations on the themes of ignorance and compulsion.

Mental illness, however, is a problem for Aristotle's scheme. An old controversy in jurisprudence revolves around whether mental illness is itself an excuse from responsibility, or whether mental illness excuses only insofar as it is a subclass of another excusing condition, such as ignorance or compulsion. In fact, neither position gives us an adequate account of the relationship between mental illness and a person's responsibility for his actions. In some cases a person's mental illness may be such that when he acted, he acted in ignorance or under compulsion. A delusion, for instance, may have caused him to believe that he was doing something else. But in other cases a person may be so mentally disordered, so psychotic or demented that we cannot even consider him a morally responsible agent. In these cases we cannot ascribe to that person those mental characteristics, such as intentions, which we normally assume of the mentally sound. In these cases, I argue, the mentally disordered person lies outside our scheme of moral responsibility entirely.

Chapters 3 through 6 all concern, in their different ways, relatively specific sorts of mental disorder. Chapter 3 deals with what I call the "volitionally disordered offender," by which I mean offenders who have acted under the sway of aberrant desires, desires that to most of us seem peculiar even in their best light, and that often seem frankly bizarre: the kleptomaniac who shoplifts worthless trinkets, the frotteur who rubs against unsuspecting women in the subway, the necrophiliac, the exhibitionist, and the pyromaniac. I outline a way of approaching these offenders based loosely on the notion of duress. If we regard these volitionally disordered persons as having acted under duress, then some of them may be less blameworthy than they first appear.

Chapter 4 focuses on questions of responsibility and character — questions of particular importance in people with personality disorders. I argue against the notion that the reason we excuse mentally disordered persons is that they are not morally bad people, and I suggest that, in general, persons with personality disorders must be held morally responsible for their actions, as long as they have acted intentionally. The one possible exception to this rule — the psychopath — is discussed in chapter 5. There, I explore the notion of what it means to understand morality, arguing that the psychopath is capable of some limited degree of moral understanding, but that his deficiencies leave him incapable of the richer engagement with morality that is necessary for full moral understanding and full responsibility for one's actions.

Chapter 6 concerns the relationship between responsibility and a person's beliefs. This relationship becomes especially important in persons who are psychotically deluded — for instance, persons with schizophrenia, bipolar affective disorder, or psychotic depression. Such persons may not actually be doing what they think they are doing, and for this reason they might be excused on grounds of ignorance. I also explore the case of persons who suffer radical, temporary psychological changes; if these changes are severe enough, we might in some cases regard the person as having become, from a moral point of view, a "different" person.

However, some persons have mental disorders so severe that we can no longer regard them as morally responsible agents. In chapter 7, I argue that, as with small children, we cannot include these people in our scheme of responsibility. I criticize rationality as a criterion for morally responsible agency, and I suggest alternative approaches for making such judgments.

In discussing all of these various mental disorders, I have tried to include case histories that illuminate the points that I am trying to make. But there are certainly many disorders that I have not addressed here, and many further variations on the ones that I have included. The ones that I have discussed are not meant to exhaust all discussion, of course, but rather to provide a general approach for judging the broader spectrum of psychiatric problems.

Finally, a few words of explanation. Language is constantly evolving, and certain terms come in and out of fashion. At various points in the book I use the terms "mentally ill," "mentally disordered," "psychiatrically ill," and probably a few others. In lieu of a debate on which term is better, what counts as "illness" and so on, let me just say that in general, by all of these terms I am referring loosely to the sort of person whose problems would bring her to the attention of a psychiatrist.

I am also conscious both of the need to avoid using gender-exclusive pronouns such as "he," "him," "his," and so on, and of the need to avoid cumbersome combinations such as "his or her" or "he/she." My compromise has been to alternate, in a somewhat random fashion, between using male and female pronouns.

I should also note that this is not a book about legal responsibility. Questions of legal responsibility take into their scope a broad spectrum of questions that are peripheral to the question of moral responsibility — questions about the purpose of the law, about punishment, about legal procedure. The question that I want to address is strictly that of moral responsibility: determining when a mentally disordered person deserves the moral credit for what he has done. This often overlaps with questions of legal responsibility, and occasionally I turn briefly to legal points by way of comparison or contrast. However, my focus is mainly on the moral.

Any approach based on particulars will leave a number of areas and issues unexamined. This book is no exception. I have chosen to focus on the sorts of mental disorder that exemplify best the types of problems that are most important for responsibility, with the hope that my discussion of these will provide a framework within which the problems of other mental disorders can be understood. Because contemporary Western society has developed relatively consistent and uncontroversial ways of judging the moral responsibility of ordinary human beings for their actions, I have taken my bearings from these ordinary judgments of responsibility. We can travel a long way toward understanding our attitudes regarding the mentally disordered by examining our attitudes regarding ordinary human beings.

1

Insanity Pleas: Mental Disorders and Legal Responsibility

Toward the close of *The Brothers Kara-mazov,* Ivan Karamazov, on the verge of an attack of brain fever, is visited by a genteel but shabby gentleman whom he understands to be the Devil. Ivan questions him about the tortures that the other world has in store, and he receives this reply:

> What tortures? Ah, don't ask. In the old days we had all sorts, but now they are chiefly moral punishments — the "stings of conscience" and all that nonsense. We got that, too, from you, from the softening of your manners. And who's the better for it? Only those who have no conscience, for how can they be tortured by conscience when they have none? But decent people who have conscience and a sense of honor suffer. Reforms, when the ground has not been prepared for them, especially if they have been copied from abroad, cause nothing but trouble. The ancient fire was better.

This book is about the stings of conscience, rather than the ancient fire. It concerns issues of moral responsibility, not legal responsibility, and concepts such as blame, rather than punishment. That which accompanies judgments of moral responsibility cannot replace that which accompanies judgments of legal responsibility, as Dostoyevsky's old gentleman implies, but

9

neither should the two sorts of judgments be confused. Morality and the law have different agendas.

Nonetheless, when a mentally disordered person acts in a way that is morally or legally wrong, he is apt eventually to come into contact with the courts, and with a psychiatrist. It is unlikely that he will ever see a moral philosopher. The dispensation of mentally disordered criminal offenders is not merely a conceptual problem; it is a practical problem involving matters such as psychiatric treatment, punishment, and confinement. Because psychiatrists and attorneys are most intimately involved in these practical affairs — and because, unlike morality, the law can be changed with the stroke of a pen — it should not be surprising that, historically, much more attention has been given to the question of the legal responsibility of the mentally disordered than to the matter of their moral responsibility.

Their differences notwithstanding, judgments of moral and legal responsibility are closely tied, and the law's long and controversial history of dealing with mentally disordered offenders proves a fertile source of instruction for a moral analysis. Unlike morality, the law has been set the task of developing explicit rules of insanity, guidelines by which it is determined who is sane and therefore should be held accountable for his or her actions, and who is insane and therefore must be exonerated. This chapter traces some of the controversies that have emerged in the development of various insanity pleas, as well as some of the difficulties associated with their application and interpretation.

The M'Naghten Rules

By far the most influential, the most widely quoted, and the most roundly criticized tests of legal insanity are the M'Naghten Rules. In 1843, Daniel M'Naghten of Glasgow shot and killed Edward Drummond, the secretary to the prime minister, Robert Peel. M'Naghten shot Drummond in broad daylight, literally with a police officer at his elbow. Deluded that he was being persecuted by a number of people in England and Scotland, including the Tory government, M'Naghten had intended to kill Peel, and indeed, after the act thought he had done so. M'Naghten was tried and acquitted by reason of insanity.

The political climate at the time of M'Naghten was stormy, and the Queen had recently been the object of an assassination attempt for which the failed assassin was acquitted by reason of insanity. For this reason, the House of Lords asked the judges in M'Naghten's trial to explain the tests by which a person could be properly judged criminally insane. Out of these hearings emerged the M'Naghten Rules. In their essence the rules state:

The jurors ought to be told in all cases that every man is to be presumed to be sane, and to possess a sufficient degree of reason to be responsible for his crimes, until the contrary be proved to their satisfaction; and that to establish a defense on the grounds of insanity, it must be conclusively proved that, at the time of committing the act, the party accused was laboring under such a defect of reason, from the disease of the mind, as not to know the nature and quality of the act he was doing; or if he did know it, that he did not know what he was doing was wrong.[1]

The shadow cast by M'Naghten has been long, not only in the United Kingdom but also in the United States, Canada, Australia, and New Zealand. With its influence, however, has come widespread criticism. In the voluminous literature on M'Naghten, the most common criticisms relevant to moral responsibility relate to its focus on deficits in reasoning ability and to the vagueness of the language it employs.

The M'Naghten Rules state explicitly that criminal insanity must depend on whether the party accused labors under a "defect of reason." Critics of M'Naghten have argued that this emphasis on reason is based on the faulty assumption that cognition is the only or the most important mental capacity relevant to responsibility. This assumption, in turn, implies the further false assumption that the mind can be separated into compartments — for example, cognition, emotion, and volition — and that cognition is the most important determinant of behavior. The Butler Committee Report on Mentally Abnormal Offenders (1975) argued that:

> The main defect of the M'Naghten test is that it was based on the now obsolete belief in the pre-eminent role of reason in controlling social behavior. It therefore requires evidence of the cognitive capacity, in particular the knowledge and understanding of the defendant at the time of the act or omission charged. Contemporary psychiatry and psychology emphasize that man's social behavior is determined more by how he has learned to behave than by what he knows or understands.[2]

Even if it were possible to compartmentalize mental functions into various faculties, this criticism of the M'Naghten test emphasizes another important point: a person's affect or mood is also relevant to responsibility, because a person's mood may color how he perceives his actions, and thus what he believes about them. Critics also point out that a person may understand his actions but for some reason be unable to control them. M'Naghten ignores self-control, perhaps as a result of the tacit assumption that a person's powers of self-control are strengthened by the knowledge that lapses will be punished.[3]

This perceived deficiency in M'Naghten was important in shaping a subsequent test of criminal insanity, the so-called irresistible impulse test.

The language of M'Naghten is also a target of frequent criticism. For example, it is unclear what qualifies as a "disease of the mind." Must this be an organic disease? This would exclude most of the sorts of problem that psychiatrists and psychologists treat, the so-called functional disorders. If it includes functional disorders, must these be severe psychoses, or does the rubric also encompass disorders outside the bounds of psychosis — affective disorders, for example, such as depression? What about dementia and mental retardation?

Psychotic illness seems to be the paradigm for an insanity defense, but many other mental impairments appear to fall on M'Naghten's borders. According to Goldstein and Marcus, actual judicial cases in the United States are silent as to what qualifies as mental illness. In general, nonpsychotic mental illness does not seem to qualify, but mental retardation qualifies if it deprives the defendant of the knowledge specified in M'Naghten.[4] On the other hand, even though the law does not define "disease of the mind," or mental illness, the insanity defense has been successfully invoked for a broad variety of cases, including fugue states, amnesia, post-traumatic stress disorder, somnambulism, and automatisms.[5]

Similar criticisms are directed at another ambiguity in M'Naghten, its stipulation that a person "not know the nature and quality of the act he was doing." Some have taken issue with the verb "know," arguing that it implies a rigid, shallow, intellectual understanding. A mentally ill person may possess this sort of understanding but lack the fuller, richer, more emotionally charged understanding that healthy persons have. This narrow definition of "know" restricts those eligible for an insanity defense, in Zilboorg's graphic phrase, to the "totally deteriorated, drooling, hopeless psychotics of long-standing, and congenital idiots."[6]

The "nature and quality of the act" is a phrase that has caused similar confusion. Some have taken it to mean merely the brute physical character of the act: a person must realize that it is a person he is shooting at and not a stump, that he has a gun in his hand and not a banana, and so on. Others argue that the knowledge of the nature and quality of some acts must include some idea of what it is like to be the victim of that act. That is, a person cannot be said to understand causing a person physical pain if he is incapable of empathy, of appreciating the position of the person who is experiencing the pain. Some have argued as well that the nature and quality of an act must also include an appreciation of the moral and legal significance of the act.

The final provision of the act, and potentially the most problematic, is that a person may be acquitted by reason of insanity if he did not know that his act was wrong. First, it is debatable whether this provision belongs in an insanity defense. Some see it as a license to exonerate offenders who feel no guilt or remorse for their misdeeds. Second, if the provision is included, it is not clear whether the provision should mean legally wrong or morally wrong. If the latter, then the test is subject to a number of problems about what it might mean not to know that an action is morally wrong.

But holding "wrong" to mean "legally wrong" has its problems as well. One of these problems, as the Committee on Mentally Abnormal Offenders noted, is that ignorance of the criminal law is not a defense available to sane offenders.[7] It might be argued that the knowledge of right and wrong to which M'Naghten refers is knowledge of the moral beliefs generally held by the members of a given society. But this sort of knowledge becomes problematic with actions that are legally prohibited, but are widely held to be morally acceptable, such as rational suicide or active euthanasia.[8] It is also unclear how this sort of interpretation would apply to actions that a person believes to be morally acceptable but that she realizes that society regards as morally wrong.

Irresistible Impulse Test

Perhaps because of the failure of the M'Naghten Rules to include a provision in their definition of insanity for volitional control, later tests of insanity began to mention volition as a relevant factor in criminal responsibility. Commonly known as the "irresistible impulse" test, this standard allowed a defendant to be exonerated from legal responsibility if it could be shown that he was unable to control his actions. In his *History of the Criminal Law of England* (1883), Fitzjames Stephen wrote that an action should not be considered a crime if the agent was "prevented either by defective mental power or by any disease affecting his mind from controlling his own conduct, unless the absence of the power of control has been produced by his own fault."[9]

Though it was much debated, the irresistible impulse test was never adopted in England. However, it was invoked in a number of cases in the United States. For example, *Parsons v. State* (1887) ruled that even if a person had knowledge of right and wrong, he might nevertheless be excused from legal responsibility if the following conditions applied:

1. If, by reason of the duress of such mental disease, he has so far lost the power to choose between the right and the wrong, and to avoid doing the act in question, as that his free agency was destroyed;

2. And if, at the same time, the alleged crime was so connected with such mental disease, in the relation of cause and effect, as to have been the product of it solely.[10]

Contrary to what its name suggests, the irresistible impulse test is not a test of impulsiveness. A desire may be irresistible, but not impulsive. The point of the test is to excuse a person from responsibility for his action if he could not prevent himself from acting — that is, if he could not control his behavior.

However, the primary problem with the irresistible impulse test should be obvious. That is, it is impossible to distinguish between behavior that the agent *did* not control and behavior that the agent *could* not control. Merely because a person has not prevented himself from acting does not mean that he was unable to prevent himself from acting. As the American Psychiatric Association's 1983 position paper on the insanity defense pointed out: "The line between an irresistible impulse and an impulse not resisted is probably no sharper than that between twilight and dusk."[11] To distinguish between the two can be difficult.

The Durham Rule

The Durham rule was established in the United States District of Columbia in 1954. In *Durham v. United States,* Judge David Bazelon ruled that "an accused is not criminally responsible if his unlawful act was the product of a mental disease or defect."[12] Bazelon instructed the jury:

> If you the jury believe beyond a reasonable doubt that the accused was not suffering from a diseased or defective mental condition at the time he committed the criminal act charged, you may find him guilty. If you believe he was suffering from a diseased or defective mental condition when he committed the act, but believe beyond a reasonable doubt that the act was not the product of such mental abnormality, you may find him guilty. Unless you believe beyond a reasonable doubt either that he was not suffering from a diseased or defective mental condition, or that the act was not the product of such abnormality, you must find the accused not guilty by reason of insanity. Thus your task would not be completed upon finding, if you did, that the accused suffered from a mental disease or defect. He would still be responsible for his unlawful act if there was no causal connection between such abnormality and the act. These questions must be determined by you from the facts which you find to be fairly deducible from the testimony and the evidence in this case.[13]

The important differences between the Durham rule and the M'Naghten Rules were twofold. First, the Durham rule spoke of the defendant's "mental disease or defect," rather than the "defect of reason" of M'Naghten. Second, the Durham rule stipulated that for an insanity plea to be successful, the criminal act must have been the *product* of the accused's mental abnormality. One purpose of the Durham rule was to shift from the narrow emphasis of M'Naghten on reason to a broader, more integrated model of human personality. It was thought that this change would allow psychiatrists to testify more freely about the broad range of factors relevant to the defendant's mental condition.[14] Psychiatry rarely concerns itself with questions about defects of reason, or knowing the difference between right and wrong. Durham allowed testimony from psychiatrists on much broader issues, with the hope that juries would thus be better informed to make judgments about the defendant's mental life.[15]

Though the Durham rule was not established until 1954, the ideas that led to its adoption had been debated for some time. A law similar to Durham had been adopted in New Hampshire in 1869 as a result of the writings of the Maine physician Isaac Ray.[16] In contrast to the narrow criteria of M'Naghten, Ray believed that a person should be exonerated by reason of insanity as long as his mental abnormality embraced the criminal act within its sphere of influence.[17] These ideas found their way into law in *State v. Pike,* which stated that the defendant in a murder trial should be acquitted if "the killing was the offspring or product of mental disease."[18]

Ray's ideas were debated extensively in England, but were never adopted. In 1923, the Medico-Psychological Association proposed to the Atkin Committee on Insanity and Crime that the M'Naghten Rules be replaced by a formulation similar to that which Ray advocated. The Atkin Committee eventually recommended a more conservative position advocated by the British Medical Association, which proposed that the irresistible impulse test be added to the M'Naghten Rules, but the government favored neither proposal and did not make any changes to the existing law.[19]

In the United States, the Durham rule proved to be unsuccessful for several reasons. First, because it widened the range of relevant mental abnormalities without offering any definition of what constituted "mental disease or defect," it opened the door for debates between psychiatrists about the definition of mental disease, and the pertinence of conditions such as psychopathy and narcotics addiction.[20]

Second, because of its stipulation that the accused's action be the product of mental disease or defect, Durham gave rise to irresolvable disputes over mental causation. According to Durham, the presence of mental illness was not an excuse in itself; it excused only if it in some way caused the defendant's action. However, this distinction is in practice of little value, because it is extremely difficult to argue that the actions of a mentally ill person are in no way caused by his mental illness.[21]

The courts initially invited testimony from psychiatrists and psychologists about the relationship between the defendant's mental condition and his offense. However, it gradually became clear that this was in fact an invitation for experts to expound on their opinions of the defendant's moral culpability. By 1967, the courts had directly prohibited any psychiatric testimony about whether the defendant's action was the product of his disease.[22]

Moore argues persuasively that this failure was to be expected, given the clash between the deterministic assumptions of psychiatry and the law's assumptions of free will. While the law must assume that a person acts freely unless it is shown otherwise, psychiatry diagnoses and treats mental illness by assuming that there is a cause of the mentally ill person's thoughts and behavior. Moore notes, "If mentally ill persons are excused because of their lack of 'free will' (in a contra-causal sense), then psychiatry could be of no help, for its theoretical commitment is that none of us enjoys the freedom the mentally ill are supposed to lack."[23]

The American Law Institute Model Penal Code

In 1962, the American Law Institute proposed its Model Penal Code, whose section on the insanity defense read:

1. A person is not responsible for criminal conduct if at the time of such conduct as a result of mental disease or defect he lacks the substantial capacity either to appreciate the criminality (wrongfulness) of his conduct or to conform his conduct to the requirements of law;

2. As used in this article, the terms "mental disease" or "defect" do not include an abnormality manifested only by repeated criminal or anti-social conduct.[24]

The A.L.I. test was an attempt to remedy many of the difficulties of earlier formulations of the insanity defense. By saying that to be held responsible an agent must have the capacity "to conform his conduct" to the law, the A.L.I. test covered some of the difficulties in volitional control which the irresistible impulse test was designed to handle. By substituting "appreciate" for M'Naghten's "know," the A.L.I. test was intended to convey a deeper and less narrowly intellectual sense of understanding. In a fashion similar to M'Naghten, the A.L.I. test focused on the defendant's ability to appreciate wrongfulness, and it also included a clause clearly intended to exclude the diagnosis of psychopathic or sociopathic personality from the definition of mental disease. And like Durham, by including the stipulation that the act be "the result of" mental disease or defect, the A.L.I. test retained the need for a causal connection between the mental abnormality and the crime.[25]

However, the A.L.I. test also retains some of the problems of its predecessors: what is meant by mental disease; how to tell whether a person is truly incapable of conforming his conduct to the law or whether he merely did not conform it; what is meant by "criminality" or "wrongfulness"; and what it means to "appreciate" criminality or wrongfulness. Moreover, like Durham, it has the problematic requirement that an action be caused by mental disease.

Another potential difficulty is created by the A.L.I. test's stipulation that the criteria should not apply to abnormalities manifested only by repeated criminal or antisocial conduct. This stipulation was presumably meant to exclude the so-called "psychopath," or "sociopath," or "antisocial personality," whose condition has often been included in psychiatric diagnostic schemes but who many people also feel should be held accountable for his actions. However, the A.L.I.'s stipulation might well also exclude some other offenders from the insanity defense whom many people would regard as properly falling within its scope. For example, a person with an organic frontal lobe lesion might exhibit only disinhibited behavior; such a person would be suffering from an illness for which she bears no responsibility, but which is manifested only in antisocial behavior. Many people would regard such a person as not responsible for her actions, but, at least on its surface, the A.L.I. code would seem to exclude her from using the insanity defense.[26]

Diminished Responsibility

Because of its historical reliance on the defense of "diminished capacity," Scotland escaped many of the snares and pitfalls that persistently reappeared in English and American jurisprudence. This defense allowed for a middle road between the verdict of sane and guilty on the one hand, and that of insane and excusable on the other. If her mental faculties were partially impaired, a person's criminal responsibility could be mitigated. The originator of the diminished capacity defense, Sir George Mackenzie of Rosenhaugh (1636–69), wrote:

> It might be argued that since the law grants a total impunity to such as are absolutely furious therefore should by the rule of proportions lessen and moderate the punishments of such, as though they are not absolutely mad yet are Hypochondrick and Melancholy to such a degree, that it clouds their reason.[27]

Scotland's "diminished responsibility" defense eventually made its way into English law, when a version of it was included in the Homicide Act 1957. This law stated:

> Where a person kills, or is party to the killing of another, he shall not be convicted of murder if he was suffering from such abnormality of mind (whether arising from a condition of arrested or retarded development of mind or any inherent causes or induced by disease or injury) as substantially impaired his mental responsibility for his acts and omissions in doing or being party to the killing.[28]

The Homicide Act 1957 had obvious deficiencies in its confusing language, with terms such as "mental responsibility" and "abnormality of mind." Nonetheless, from a moral standpoint, the "diminished responsibility" standard is a sensible one. First, it conforms with our common sense notions of causation; there are often many causes to an event, of which the agent's action is only one. Thus, from this graded concept of causal responsibility seems to follow a graded concept of moral responsibility. Second, the borderline between mentally ill and mentally healthy is not always bright. A defense of diminished responsibility aligns more truly with a picture of mental capacity painted in shades of gray, rather than black and white. The Royal Commission on Capital Punishment 1949–53 made this observation:

> It must be accepted that there is no dividing line between sanity and insanity, but that the two extremes of "sanity" and "insanity" shade into one another by imperceptible gradations. The degree of individual responsibility varies equally widely; no clear boundary can be drawn between responsibility and irresponsibility. . . . The acceptance of the doctrine of diminished responsibility would undoubtedly bring the law into closer harmony with the facts and would enable the courts to avoid passing sentence of death in numerous cases in which it will not be carried out.[29]

Conclusion

From a moral perspective, two broad points about the various formulations of the insanity defense are worth considering. The first point concerns the disputes over the definition of mental illness and its causal relationship to the defendant's action. In previous years, much of the debate over the various formulations of the insanity defense centered around the question of how mental aberrations and deficiencies were related to a person's actions. Certain sorts of mental problems seemed clearly unrelated, yet others were obviously highly relevant; the point at issue was to try to establish some sort of definition that included the relevant problems and excluded the others. Thus came endless debate over the terms "mental disease," "mental defect," "mental abnormality," "defect of reason," and so on.

The debate over causation arose for similar reasons. One did not want mental illness to be an excuse in itself; this would mean that even mental illnesses with no bearing at all on a person's actions would excuse him from responsibility. The solution to this was to require some sort of causal relationship between the mental illness and the action, to require that the action be the "product" or the "result" of the mental illness. But this engendered futile arguments about causal relationships between mental illness and action (arguments that were, and are, thought to be empirical, but that are in fact philosophical).

Both of these debates arise from a faulty theoretical model of the mind and how it relates to responsibility. This model supposes that responsibility is absent if an identifiable physical cause of the agent's actions can be found. Much of the search for an acceptable definition of the sorts of mental illness which abrogate responsibility is an effort to include organic mental disorders and those for which an organic or physical cause is suspected — those disorders that might be more properly regarded as neurological, rather than psychiatric — and to exclude the less physically explainable functional disorders. The assumption is that if the action has a physical cause, then responsibility is negated, because the agent did not "will" or "intend" the action. We are responsible only for those actions that are caused by our willing them, and if it can be shown that they are in fact caused by a physical brain abnormality, then the agent can no longer be held responsible for the action.

This model ignores the fact that we have (at least) two different languages in which to speak about mental events, and that speaking in one language does not exclude the possibility of speaking in the other. On the one hand, we speak of the brain, its anatomy and its physiology, of tumors causing personality changes and neurotransmitter deficiencies causing hallucinations. On the other hand, we speak of the will and intentions, of having reasons for actions, of actions resulting from beliefs and desires. However, identifying a mental illness in physical language and pointing to it as the "cause" of an action does not mean that this other language of will and intention no longer applies. Identifying the cause of a person's action in physical terms does not mean that the agent did not "will" that action. A person who acts violently as a result of a tumor may have willed his violent action just as much as a person with a healthy, normal brain. This is not to say, of course, that we do not have good reason to exonerate mentally ill offenders for their actions, especially the violent person with a brain tumor. It is only to say that the reason for exonerating them is not that we have identified a "cause" for the action which negates intention or will.[30]

Clarifying this confusion eliminates the problems of determining what qualifies as a mental illness, and whether mental illness has caused the agent's actions. It quickly becomes clear that these are not the relevant questions. What we actually want to know, and what these questions are in fact pointing to, are whether the mental disorder is to a significant degree *relevant* to the agent's action, and whether the agent is *responsible* for this disorder. The causation clauses in the insanity defenses are attempts to cover the first of these; we do not want to allow mental disorders that clearly have no bearing on a person's action to negate her responsibility for that action. The definitions of mental illness were attempts to deal with the second of these; we do not want to excuse a person from responsibility if her mental illness was something for which she was to some degree responsible, such as a flawed character.

The second point concerns an area of confusion in these formulations of the insanity defense about the *reason* why insanity might excuse a person from responsibility for his actions. Throughout these formulations, a tension exists between two approaches. On the one hand, the formulations sometimes seem to assume that insanity excuses in the way that ignorance or compulsion excuse. That is, if insanity in some way negates or alters the agent's intention, then he is excused from responsibility. In this view, insanity might cause a person to be ignorant in some way about what he is doing, or it might compel him in some way to act, and its influence in either of these cases might negate the agent's intentions and hence his responsibility. Thus arose the ideas that an agent might be excused if he did not appreciate the wrongfulness of his action, if he could not conform his conduct to the law, and so on.

On the other hand, at other times the formulations seem to be operating under the assumption that insanity creates a special *class of beings,* the members of which cannot be regarded as morally responsible for their actions. In the same way that, for example, infants and animals cannot be regarded as morally responsible for their actions, neither can the insane, and the task of an insanity defense is to determine which persons belong in this class of the insane. This assumption seems to underlie M'Naghten's emphasis on a defect of reason as the distinguishing characteristic of insanity. It is not that a defect of reason negates intention; it is that a defect of reason marks out a person as belonging to the class of beings who cannot be regarded as responsible for their actions.

There is merit in each of these views of the insanity defense. In some cases, we are inclined to say that the reason for excusing a person from responsibility is that his mental illness negates his intentions, as when a delusion causes a person to believe that he is doing something other than what he is actually doing (say, shooting at a body-snatcher rather than at his nephew).[31] In other cases, we are inclined to say that a person should be exonerated because he is not sufficiently like other humans beings for us to regard him as such for the purposes of assessing responsibility. A severe psychotic or a patient with Alzheimer's disease might fall into this class of beings.[32] Though I will argue later that we must incorporate both of these two conceptions into our ideas of how mental illness negates moral responsibility, for the moment it is sufficient to note that the tension between these two conceptions of how insanity excuses lies at the root of many of the problems with previous formulations of the insanity defense.

In this chapter, I have tried to give a brief overview of the issues involved in the insanity defense, especially those issues related to moral responsibility. By this point it should be clear that a major problem for the insanity defense is the fact that different types of mental disorder can affect a person's moral and legal responsibility for his actions in very different ways. The difficulty is that of encompassing the common elements of a wide variety of disorders within a few understandable formulations. This is also a difficulty for the questions of moral responsibility, and not just for those people who are mentally disordered. One of the aims of the next chapter, which draws on Aristotle, will be to sort out in a broader fashion the various ways in which a person might be excused from responsibility for his actions.

2

Mental Illness, Aristotle, and the Straight Rule of Responsibility

How we assess the responsibility of the mentally disordered is inseparable from how we assess the responsibility of the mentally sound. Moral responsibility is a concept that has developed largely out of the language of social relationships between mentally sound adults, and when we judge the responsibility of the mentally disordered, it is in this much broader concept of responsibility that our judgments will be anchored. This broader scheme of responsibility is by no means free of philosophical problems, but the ground-level concepts that underlie it are fairly straightforward.

What I would like to do here is to explore some of the basic concepts underlying moral responsibility, and to draw some parallels between those concepts and the special difficulties that arise in judging the responsibility of mentally disordered persons. To do this, I want to examine what J. L. Mackie calls the "straight rule of responsibility," which grounds moral responsibility in *intentional action,* and which ultimately derives from Aristotle's work on voluntariness in the *Nicomachean Ethics.* Very often we can refine our notions of how to behave toward mentally ill persons by looking at other more familiar situations — the responsibility of children, for example, or the responsibility of mentally sound persons acting under stressful or difficult circumstances. In this chapter, I will explore the writing of Aristotle on several of these types of cases, and I will also look briefly at some of the more philosophically complex problems for responsibility, such as recklessness and responsibility for failed tries.

Aristotle, Intention, and the Involuntary

At its most basic level, responsibility hinges on a person's intentions. In general we hold people morally responsible only for those things that they have done intentionally. To say, on the other hand, that a person did not intend to act usually means that she is excused from responsibility for the action. For this reason, most excuses are a variation on the theme of nonintention, either directly ("I didn't mean to") or obliquely ("I didn't see him," "I couldn't help it").

Generally speaking, there are two types of excuse. The first is ignorance: if a person did not know what she was doing, then generally she cannot be held responsible for doing it. The second is compulsion: a person cannot be held responsible for something that she could not help doing.

Mental illness can obviously influence a person's intentions very dramatically. Those intentions can be influenced by (among others) two broad categories of disorder, which correspond to the two general types of excusing condition, ignorance and compulsion. Disorders like schizophrenia and bipolar affective disorder can affect a person's *beliefs,* and as a result, the person may be "ignorant" of what he is actually doing — say, a psychotic man with delusions of jealousy who verbally abuses the man he mistakenly believes is having an affair with his wife. On the other hand, disorders like kleptomania or exhibitionism concern a person's *desires,* and thus a disordered person may be, if not exactly "compelled" to act, at least faced with strong desire, which may mitigate that person's blame.

The credit for linking moral responsibility with intention belongs to Aristotle. Book III of the *Nicomachean Ethics* begins with the observation that it is necessary to distinguish between involuntary and voluntary actions because "on voluntary actions praise and blame are bestowed, on those that are involuntary pardon, and sometimes also pity."[1] Though Aristotle did not write specifically about responsibility, he was concerned with questions of "praise and blame," and his discussion of the "voluntary and involuntary" is often treated as an account of moral responsibility.

Aristotle's discussion in the *Nicomachean Ethics* has influenced subsequent treatments of moral responsibility in innumerable ways, but especially noteworthy are two ways in which it has set the structural terms for current discussions. First, Aristotle does not so much seek to develop an account of responsibility as he does an account of excuses. He approaches the problem of responsibility indirectly, attempting not to show what makes a person *responsible* for his actions, but rather to show what makes a person *not* responsible. In Book III of the *Nicomachean Ethics,* Aristotle focuses his attention less on what makes an action voluntary than on what makes it involuntary — and thereby excusable — and on borderline or difficult cases. This stance seems reasonable; in ordinary life we usually assume that a person has acted voluntarily unless we have reason to suspect otherwise.

Second, Aristotle outlines and explores the two main excusing conditions, ignorance and compulsion. Voluntary actions, says Aristotle, are the actions "in which the moving principle is in the agent himself, he being aware of the particular circumstances of the action."[2] In contrast, those actions are involuntary "which take place by force or owing to ignorance."[3] Thus, Aristotle implies, a person should be considered morally responsible for an action unless that action was involuntary; i.e., done in ignorance or under compulsion (force).

Compulsion

The actions of some people with psychiatric disorders are related, in a number of varied ways, to compulsions and other problems of volition. The obsessive-compulsive disorder is one obvious example; a more complicated one is that of persons with schizophrenia who experience the delusion that their actions are being controlled by others. Some persons with schizophrenia also experience command hallucinations, in which they hear voices telling them to behave in certain ways. The actions of patients with psychosexual disorders, such as exhibitionism or voyeurism, and impulse-control disorders, such as kleptomania, are related to their strong and unusual desires. The challenge in these sorts of disorders is to understand how compulsion and other disorders of volition might compromise voluntariness. A preliminary step toward this end is to see how compulsion might compromise voluntariness for the mentally sound.

Aristotle outlines a number of different situations where this might be the case. The clearest cases of compulsion, according to Aristotle, are those where the "moving principle" is "outside" the agent. Aristotle says that a person's action (or better, his movement) would be considered compelled, for example, if that person were to be carried somewhere by the wind, or by men who had that person in their power.

However, Aristotle recognizes that it is not always so clear whether an action was compelled. He cites two borderline cases of the type now known as "necessity" or "duress." In the cases, first, of the captain of a storm-battered ship who tosses goods overboard to secure the crew's safety, and second, of a person who accedes to the demands of a tyrant holding his family hostage, Aristotle says that the actions are neither voluntary nor involuntary, but rather "mixed actions."

However, Aristotle says that even though these actions are mixed, they are more like voluntary actions. He maintains that "the end of an action is relative to the occasion," and concludes that these actions are "voluntary, but in the abstract perhaps involuntary, for no one would choose such an action in itself."[4] He elaborates on this by saying that such actions "are more like voluntary acts; for actions are in the class of particulars, and the particular acts here are voluntary."[5] Even though *in general* one would not throw valuable goods into the ocean, these particular circumstances made the action reasonable, and it is to particular circumstances that we should look when we decide whether an action was involuntary.

Aristotle also realizes that it is often difficult to determine what hardships should be suffered before one chooses to act wrongfully — "what should be chosen at what cost, and what should be endured at what gain."[6] Sometimes we praise a person for enduring something painful in return for a worthy end, yet on the other hand, as Aristotle says, "to endure the greatest indignities for no noble end or for a trifling end is the mark of an inferior person."[7] Sometimes we would not go so far as to praise a person, but we would pardon him, if he acted wrongfully but under pressure that no one could be expected to withstand. This point is relevant for people with some psychosexual and impulse-control disorders, who may have very strong desires to behave in morally unacceptable ways (pedophiles, for instance). How much personal distress justifies a wrongful action? Some actions are so reprehensible, Aristotle says, that one ought to face death rather than do them.

Ignorance

More complex than Aristotle's account of compulsion is his second broad category of excusing condition, that of ignorance. This category of excuse is especially relevant to mentally disordered offenders whose disorders may impair their ability (in the words of M'Naghten) to "know the nature and quality" of their actions.

Aristotle is quick to note, however, that not all sorts of ignorance make an action involuntary. It must be ignorance of a specific type. For instance, Aristotle says that a person has not acted involuntarily if he is merely ignorant of what actions are to his advantage, or if he is ignorant of "universals." The species of ignorance that qualifies an action as involuntary is ignorance of *particulars:* "the circumstances of the action and the objects with which it is concerned."[8,9] A person might be ignorant of particulars, says Aristotle, if he were to kill his son under the false belief that he was an enemy, or if he were to stab him believing that a pointed spear had a button tip.

Aristotle also says that actions done in rage or out of drunkenness cannot be excused on grounds of ignorance. He defends this by making what sounds like a peculiar distinction. Aristotle says that although the drunken or enraged man does act *in* ignorance, he does not act by reason *of* ignorance. What Aristotle seems to be getting at is the point that even though such people do not act knowingly, they act as a result of being drunk or enraged. This sort of ignorance is culpable, because the people could have avoided getting into such a state.[10] The ignorance itself is a result of drunkenness or rage.[11] So while these agents are acting in ignorance, ignorance in this case is not an excuse, because the ignorance is itself the fault of the agent.

This position is intuitively reasonable, but it does lead to some additional problems. Aristotle makes it clear that he believes becoming drunk or enraged is voluntary, and he seems to be arguing that actions *performed* in a state of drunkenness or rage are involuntary but still culpable. The position here seems to be that a person is responsible for getting himself into a state where he does not know what will happen, *regardless* of what he actually does after that. But this leads to some counterintuitive results; for example, we usually blame the drunken driver more who kills a pedestrian than we do the one who arrives home safely, even though they were both equally responsible for getting drunk.[12]

The Intentional, the Voluntary, and the Deliberate

If moral responsibility depends on whether an action was intentional, what counts as an intentional action? This question is more complex than it sounds. Is it an intentional action if I try to do something but fail? Are the actions of children intentional? What about the actions of people who are severely psychotic or demented?

Part of the difficulty in answering these sorts of questions is ambiguity of language. For example, we ordinarily use the term "voluntary" slightly differently from the way we use the term "intentional." In English, the scope of the class of voluntary actions seems to be wider than that of intentional actions; some actions that we would not be inclined to call intentional we might nevertheless call voluntary. This ambiguity presents some problems for interpreting Aristotle's account, since it is not always clear which term is more appropriate for the meaning that Aristotle wants to convey when he uses the Greek *hekousion*.

Anscombe suggests that in the case of intentional actions, if the question "why?" is applied, the answer will give a reason for acting.[13] By Anscombe's account, one sort of action that might be called voluntary but not intentional are casual physical movements — matters of habit outside of one's immediate awareness, or movements done for no considered reason. The answer to "why?" here might be something like "I was fiddling," or "I don't know why."

Actions might also be voluntary which are done *to* one rather than *by* one if they are done with one's assent. For example, if I am shoved into a swimming pool and I do not protest or attempt to prevent this from being done, then my allowing myself to be pushed into the pool might reasonably be called voluntary, but not intentional. I did not intend for this to happen — I did not even act — but I am pleased that it did happen and I took no steps to stop it. Aristotle, however, does not ordinarily use *hekousion* to mean voluntary in this sense; he says that voluntary actions are those that originate in the agent himself.

Though the class of voluntary actions usually subsumes that of intentional actions, this is not always so. Sometimes an action might be comfortably described as intentional but not as voluntary. For instance, when a shopkeeper hands over his money at gunpoint, he does so intentionally, but unwillingly. Does he do it voluntarily? Probably not. Voluntariness still carries traces of "volunteering" — with what one *wants* to happen.

"Deliberate" actions are a further subclass of intentional action: those that were weighed, considered, perhaps even pondered over before they were performed. Aristotle draws a similar distinction when he discusses "chosen actions." Chosen actions are voluntary, but not all voluntary actions are chosen (for example, acts done in anger, or on the spur of the moment, or acts done by children and animals). The object of choice, says Aristotle, is the result of previous deliberation, and choice involves reason (rather than spirit or appetite).

The Responsibility of Children

Aristotle states at the outset of Book III that praise and blame are bestowed on voluntary actions, and we have seen that he considers the actions of children and animals to be within the domain of the voluntary. But is it plausible to attribute children and animals with responsibility for their actions? If so, this would be grounds for arguing that at least some mentally disordered persons ought to be held responsible as well, since many of them — even the severely disordered — arguably have more understanding of their actions than children and animals.

It is certainly true that we attribute to children and animals *some* degree of responsibility for their actions. We praise, blame, reward, and punish both children and animals, with the primary aim (usually) of influencing their behavior, and, with children, of teaching them about morality and responsibility. But we credit neither with the same level of moral accountability that we attribute to adults. Irwin believes that Aristotle has, in effect, two theories of responsibility.[14] The simple theory of responsibility is that the agent is responsible for an action if the action is the product of his beliefs and desires; this theory counts as responsible the actions of animals and children. Aristotle's more complex theory of responsibility requires that an action be the voluntary action of a creature capable of *deliberation,* and this will implicitly exclude animals and children.

Now, there are arguments for adopting either of these positions. If the purpose of a scheme of moral responsibility is to influence behavior by the assignation of praise, punishment, and so on, then it may be reasonable to include as players in the scheme any creatures whose behavior is likely to be influenced. On the other hand, it is probably unreasonable to ascribe moral responsibility to beings that are unable to appreciate the moral significance of their actions. Many philosophers have argued that psychopaths are incapable of understanding morality, for example, and certainly many severely psychotic patients are not capable of understanding even the most basic and rudimentary aspects of their actions. Aristotle himself believed that it was inappropriate to speak of moral virtue when praising a being incapable of choice and deliberation.

Nussbaum argues that the two accounts of responsibility Irwin attributes to Aristotle are not alternative attempts at a single idea, but rather two related notions with complementary functions in Aristotle's ethical theory.[15] The development of the child's capacity to deliberate about values is a slow and gradual process, and Aristotle is concerned with how children might be educated so that they will become capable of leading good lives in accordance with their own choices. The simple theory of responsibility is an "account of the animal basis for certain ethical attitudes and practices that are central in the development of an animal creature towards deliberate choice."[16] Praise and blame for the actions of beings capable of voluntary but not deliberate action are not simply methods of brute behavioral manipulation, but are rather attempts to communicate with beings able to modify their view of the good, and to persuade them to reach out toward more appropriate objects. The complex theory of responsibility is a way of making serious moral judgments about adults whose character and ways of living have been formed, while the simple theory is a means of delivering weaker assessments about beings incapable of making true choices, but who satisfy the less stringent criteria for acting voluntarily.

Responsibility and Character

A longstanding dispute in discussions of responsibility concerns the degree to which a person can be held responsible for his character. Aristotle's position on this question was clear: he believed that a person is responsible for his character, because a person makes his character by his actions.

But perhaps a man is the kind of man not to take care. Still they are themselves by their slack lives responsible for becoming men of that kind, and men are themselves responsible for being unjust or self-indulgent, in that they cheat or spend their time in drinking-bouts and the like; for it is activities exercised on particular objects that make the corresponding character. This is plain from the case of people training for any contest or action; they practice the activity the whole time. Now not to know that it is from the exercise of activities on particular objects that states of character are produced is the mark of a thoroughly senseless person.[17]

The position that Aristotle takes on responsibility for character is a controversial one, of course, and we shall return to this controversy later. The problem, briefly put, is that in many ways we are clearly *not* responsible for our characters, at least not as completely as Aristotle implies, and thus, in judging the responsibility of a person for her actions, we must find a way of accounting for those aspects of her character over which she plainly had little control, such as her genetic inheritance and upbringing.

Aristotle does in fact consider the suggestion that our constitution at birth determines our characters. However, his response is not particularly satisfying. Aristotle says merely that if vice is out of our power, then virtue is out of our power as well. This is true, of course, and contemporary public debate does often gloss over the point that if we are willing to forego blaming the criminal who has been raised in unfortunate circumstances, we ought also to refrain from praising the hero whose upbringing chance has favored. But pointing out this inconsistency does not solve the problem; it merely compounds it.

Glover suggests that the problem with Aristotle's view is the ambiguity of our concept of character.[18] Sometimes we speak of the relationship between actions and character as if it were a *causal* relationship, and at other times as if it were a *logical* one. We sometimes explain a person's actions by reference to his character — "his generous nature makes him help other people" — as if there were a causal link between his character and his actions. On the other hand, we sometimes act as if a person's character can be identified only through his actions, so that the link between character and actions is a logical one. In this sense, saying that a person has a bad character is simply another way of saying that he often acts badly.

Now if Aristotle is thinking of the relationship between action and character in the latter sense — a self-indulgent man, say, is just a man who often acts self-indulgently — then his assertion that we are responsible for our characters amounts to little more than saying that we are responsible for our actions. However, it is more likely that Aristotle is assuming what we generally assume today: that character is more than the sum of our actions. In Book II, for example, he speaks of having appropriate motives for one's actions, having an emotional disposition to find the right actions pleasant, and so on. Furthermore, he seems to believe that we build up the appropriate emotional dispositions by acting rightly and inappropriate ones by acting wrongly. If we act badly for long enough, we will be unable to act well (though we will still be culpable, since we are at fault for getting ourselves into that state). Aristotle's claim that our actions make our characters seems to be a claim about a causal process.

It is certainly not uncommon to make appraisals of character apart from appraisals of actions; in fact, this is the norm. Sometimes these appraisals are quasi-aesthetic judgments, as when we say that a person is envious. Others are more like judgments of authenticity. I might say, for example, that a person *acts* very kindly, but that I do not think that, deep down, he is a kind person.

Clearly, Aristotle maintains that we are kind, or just, or self-indulgent because of our past activities. As Glover notes, however, this leaves open the question of the cause of these prior activities. And the ultimate starting-point of this causal chain will probably be a combination of events over which we have no control.

These considerations do not generally concern Aristotle. He focuses primarily on those situations where we are called upon to weigh responsibility, rather than with the background assumptions underlying the overall picture. To some degree, this approach is consonant with present-day pragmatism. We make judgments of moral responsibility, and we will continue to do so regardless of the debates over free will, psychological determinism, and responsibility for character. We can see that inheritance and upbringing influence behavior, but that so do praise and blame, reward and punishment. Aristotle's concern is how to determine moral responsibility given the basic framework that we already have.

The Straight Rule of Responsibility

A modern version of Aristotle's account of responsibility, and one that is fairly representative of contemporary moral thinking, is the "straight rule of responsibility," so named by J. L. Mackie.[19] The straight rule states that a person should be held morally responsible for all and only his intentional actions. The straight rule subsumes Aristotle's excusing conditions of ignorance and compulsion under the rubric of "intentional actions." Actions that are compelled or done in ignorance are not intentional, and thus agents who are compelled to act or who act in ignorance are not responsible.

To see how a lack of intention excuses, it is important to realize that an action may be intentional under some descriptions but unintentional under others. If I take another person's jacket under the mistaken impression that it is mine, I have intentionally taken a jacket, but I have not intentionally taken another person's jacket. Assuming, then, that my ignorance about the jacket is itself nonculpable, then I am not morally responsible for taking this other person's jacket, because I have not taken it intentionally.

This straightforward case is one where ignorance precludes intention, and it concerns ignorance about the particular facts of an action. More problematic is ignorance of a broader nature, such as ignorance that one's action is morally wrong. Aristotle dismisses ignorance such as this, maintaining that it is only ignorance of "particulars" which excuses. Mackie disagrees: "If Eichmann believed that everything that he did was his patriotic duty, he did not intentionally do anything wrong, though we may judge that what he did intentionally was wrong."[20]

There may not be as much disagreement between Mackie and Aristotle as it appears. Mackie's point is that a person who does not believe his action to be wrong does not intentionally do wrong. But Aristotle's point may only be that this does not matter; the action is still wrong. Whichever position one takes, however, it should be clear that whatever moral credit Eichmann's actions carried belongs to Eichmann; he is undoubtedly morally responsible for his actions. Thus, the issue in dispute is not one of responsibility, but whether Eichmann's genuine belief that he was acting rightly means that his actions were morally acceptable.

Actions that are physically compelled are also not intentional. Aristotle's examples of compulsion excuse the agent by precluding intention in this way; a person carried away by the wind or by other men has not intended his action and thus is not responsible. A more complicated question is whether actions performed under "duress" or "necessity" are also unintentional — say, the shop clerk who hands over his employer's money at gunpoint. Mackie rejects the view that these actions are unintentional, arguing that only physical compulsion or constraint make an action unintentional. Necessity and duress only complicate the description under which an action might be said to be intentional. For example (to take Aristotle's example), it is less misleading to say that the crew intentionally threw the cargo of the ship overboard in order to save the ship, than it would be to say that the crew intentionally threw the cargo overboard. However, the fact that the crew threw the cargo overboard in order to avoid a worse alternative does not mean that the action was unintentional. So the crew must be held responsible for the action under the most appropriate description.

Negligence and Recklessness

Sometimes we feel that it is necessary to hold people morally responsible for actions that they did not intend. For example, we generally blame a person who has acted negligently or recklessly, even though she has not acted intentionally. Negligence and recklessness are thus problematic for the straight rule of responsibility, which holds persons responsible only for actions that they have done intentionally.

The ill effects of negligence and recklessness must be distinguished from what Mackie calls "obliquely intended" effects of actions. Obliquely intended effects are effects that are foreseen. This is not the case with effects caused by negligence or recklessness: these are effects that the agent causes as a result of acting carelessly or thoughtlessly, but that he did not foresee as a result of his action. At most he is vaguely aware that harm might come about.

The straight rule can account for some sorts of negligence and recklessness. Even if in acting intentionally a person does not realize the particular bad effects that might result from her actions, if she knows that in acting intentionally she is also acting negligently or recklessly — that is, that harm might well ensue from her actions — she has obliquely intended to act negligently or recklessly. So if a person is intentionally driving her car very fast, vaguely realizing that harm might result and that she is thus driving recklessly, she has obliquely intended to drive recklessly. Thus, to some extent she can be held responsible, though not to the same degree as if she had intended the harm directly.

The problems that negligence and recklessness present for the straight rule are twofold. First, even if the straight rule can justify holding persons responsible for some cases of negligence and recklessness on the grounds that they "obliquely" intended to act negligently or recklessly, in ordinary life we generally assign responsibility for negligence and recklessness unevenly. We usually blame a person more if actual harm has resulted from his recklessness or negligence than we do if no harm at all has resulted. This practice runs at odds with the straight rule; if a person is responsible only for what she has done intentionally, then we should hold her responsible only for acting negligently or recklessly, irrespective of the harm that results.

Second, even in those cases where the person is aware that she is acting recklessly or negligently, she usually did not foresee, and thus did not intend, the *specific* harm that resulted. Yet we sometimes hold persons responsible for harm of this sort. Moreover, sometimes a person is not even vaguely aware that harm might result from her actions and is thus not aware that she is acting recklessly or negligently. But we occasionally hold even these sorts of persons responsible for these harmful results (sometimes on the grounds that they *should* have been aware of the possibility that this harm would result).

Mackie defends the straight rule from the difficulties presented by the first problem, the uneven distribution of blame, merely by observing that the straight rule is a more just way of distributing blame and responsibility.[21] Blaming a person for the thoughtlessness or carelessness that resulted in the harm rather than the harm itself eliminates the possibility that blame will be affected by mere chance. In contrast, blaming a person for the actual unforeseen and unintended harm that ensues means that two people who act equally recklessly or negligently may be blamed unequally, if harm has by chance come about in one instance and not in another.

Mackie deals similarly with the second problem, that of unforeseen harm. He argues that a person should be held responsible only for what he has done intentionally, which is to act recklessly or negligently, and not for causing any specific harm. A person who has caused harm while drunk should not be held responsible for causing the harm, but rather for getting himself drunk, which he did intentionally. Thus in cases of recklessness and negligence, it seems, the straight rule conflicts with ordinary practice in assigning responsibility.

However, there may be a reason for imposing a very strict standard of responsibility for unforeseen harm in cases of negligence and recklessness. As Mackie observes, in ascribing *strict* legal liability, we hold people legally responsible for harms that were not foreseen, the purpose being to encourage extremely high standards of care and attention, so that unforeseen harm might be avoided.[22] Strict standards in moral responsibility may serve the same purpose — to encourage people to take care not to engage in actions that might reasonably be suspected to result in unforeseen harm, by ascribing more blame when that unforeseen harm results.

Moreover, our judgments of responsibility for actions are often clouded by similar but distinct judgments about the agent's character. A bad person can do good things, and a good person can intend to do good things and still fail to do them. As we shall see with the question of responsibility for tries, it is important to keep these judgments separate. We may think worse of a person's character if she has acted recklessly or negligently, but this judgment does not necessarily mean that she should be held morally responsible for the harm that has resulted.

Responsibility for Tries

Sometimes a person tries to do wrong but fails. When this happens, assigning moral responsibility can be difficult; the would-be wrongdoer intended to act badly — indeed, she intentionally tried to act badly — yet she has actually *done* nothing wrong. One is inclined to think that she deserves some sort of punishment — but how can we hold her responsible when no real wrongdoing has been accomplished?

Judging a person's responsibility for tries is confused by two puzzles. The first concerns the role of luck in how an action turns out: why should we hold a person *less* responsible for a failed attempt than for a successful one, when often only the slightest of chances has made the difference between success and failure? It seems unfair to hold an intended assassin less responsible for his failed attempt at murder merely because a bullet has been deflected by a Bible in the intended victim's pocket. The second puzzle is the flip side of the first: if a try has failed, how can we hold a person morally responsible *at all?* In most cases no harm has been caused by the try; a failed assassin may have, at most, damaged a few windows with his misfired bullets. What, then, are we holding him morally responsible *for?*

One way of clarifying these puzzles is to remember that our moral assessment of a person who has tried to do wrong is confused by two separate sorts of judgment. The first sort of judgment is one of moral responsibility. A judgment of moral responsibility answers a question about the connection between an agent and the moral aspects of his action. To assess responsibility, we ask what the agent did and whether it was intentional; we generally hold a person responsible only for intentional actions.

However, we usually combine with these judgments a second sort of assessment: a moral evaluation of the agent. When we make a moral judgment about a person who has tried to do wrong, we ask not only what he is responsible for but also how this try reflects upon his character. And we are inclined to think less, morally, of a person for trying to do wrong, even if his tries have come to nothing. The mere fact that a person intends to do wrong makes us think badly of him, and thus we think badly of a person who has intentionally tried to do wrong, but failed to accomplish his evil intentions.

This distinction helps to clarify the puzzle about responsibility for tries. When we judge responsibility for failed tries, we are pulled in two directions. On the one hand, we are inclined to say that a person should be *less* responsible for failed tries than for successful ones, because when a try has failed, there is little or nothing to hold a person responsible *for*. On the other hand, even when the try has failed we think badly of the agent for trying, often just as badly as we would if he had succeeded. Thus, our moral assessment is divided by conflicting intuitions — an inclination to say that the agent is less responsible for failed actions than for successful ones, on the grounds that a person who has tried but failed has *done* nothing wrong; and an inclination to say that the agent who has tried to do evil but failed is just as bad a person as the one who has succeeded.

However, it is important to realize that as important as our moral evaluation of the agent is, it is separate from our evaluation of the agent's moral responsibility. We can only hold an agent morally responsible for actions that he has intentionally *done*. If an agent has failed in his try, then usually he has done nothing to be responsible for. Now, one might well argue that we ought to punish the failed wrongdoer anyway — because he ought to be discouraged from trying again, because punishment will deter others, or simply because someone who tries to do wrong *deserves* to be punished. But determining that someone ought to be punished is not the same as determining that he was morally responsible for an action.

Conclusion

The straight rule, which is a modification of the Aristotelian account of responsibility, is a useful guideline for assessing responsibility in most cases. Because we do best to take our bearings from the usual rather than the exceptional, the straight rule will be the standard by which I guide the arguments in following chapters. However, it is by no means without problems, some of which I have mentioned in this chapter, and many of which I will return to when I discuss the responsibility of the mentally disordered.

This chapter has set out the ways in which we generally make judgments about moral responsibility, as well as some of the areas where problems arise. Chapter 3 turns from the general to the particular. At the beginning of this chapter, I suggested that there are two broad categories of excusing conditions, ignorance and compulsion, and it is to the latter of these categories that the disorders in chapter 3 relate. These disorders concern volition: the degree to which a person can control her actions.

A Working Group of the American Psychiatric Association has expressed reservations about the relevance of volitional impairment to criminal responsibility, and it suggests that those people who fail a volitional test for insanity will also fail a cognitive-type test.[23] While this may often be the case, I will argue in chapter 3 that provisions need to be made for certain types of volitionally disordered people who would probably fail neither a volitional nor a cognitive test, but who nonetheless deserve special moral consideration.

3

Desire and Duress

Case History

A 23-year-old single woman has a three-year history of kleptomania. Her impulses to steal began when she left a department store wearing clothes that she had tried on in the changing room.[1] She describes feeling strangely pleased by this experience, and later on she began driving to shopping malls on the weekends to steal clothes. Sometimes she would steal up to $2,000 worth of clothes on a single weekend. She describes feeling a growing sense of tension prior to the act, followed by relief at not being caught, and then shame. As an act of repentance, she would usually drop the clothes off at charity centers. To control her impulses to steal she began to work long hours during the week, so that she would finish her work after the clothing shops closed. She also has a seven-year history of bulimia nervosa, averaging one binge a day.

Case History

A 30-year-old man has a sixteen-year history of voyeurism.[2] He describes a variety of voyeuristic activities, such as climbing into the ceiling of his workplace in order to look into the women's bathroom through the ventilation ducts. He would sometimes go to the beach and leave a running video camera focused on women's bodies, or find a busy public spot and follow women who were not wearing bras. These activities consume several hours of his day, despite his efforts to resist. Over the previous several months, he has begun to worry about losing his job if he is caught, but he has been unable to get rid of these desires.

Case History

In his treatise *Psychopathia Sexualis,* Krafft-Ebing describes the following case
of fetishism:[3]

A baker's assistant, aged thirty-two, single, previously of good repute,
was discovered stealing a handkerchief. In sincere remorse, he confessed
that he had stolen from eighty to ninety such handkerchiefs. He cared
only for handkerchiefs, and indeed, only for those belonging to young
women attractive to him. In his outward appearance the culprit presented
nothing peculiar. He dressed himself with much taste. His conduct was
peculiar, anxious, depressed, and unmanly, and he often lapsed into
whining and tears. Lack of self-reliance, weakness of comprehension,
and slowness of perception and reflection were noticeable. One of his
sisters was epileptic. He lived in good circumstances; never had a severe illness; was well-developed. In relating his history, he showed
weakness of memory and lack of clearness; calculation was hard for
him, though when young he learned and comprehended easily. His anxious, uncertain state of mind gave rise to a suspicion of onanism. The
culprit confessed that he had been given to this practice excessively
since his nineteenth year. For some years, as a result of this vice, he had
suffered with depression, lassitude, trembling of his limbs, pain in the
back, and disinclination for work. Frequently a depressed, anxious state
of mind came over him, in which he avoided people. He had exaggerated, fantastic notions about the results of sexual intercourse with women,
and could not bring himself to indulge in it. Of late, however, he had
thought of marriage. With great remorse and in a weak-minded way, he
now confessed that six months ago, while in a crowd, he became violently excited sexually at the sight of a pretty young girl, and was compelled to crowd up against her. He felt an impulse to compensate himself for the want of a more complete satisfaction of his sexual excitement,
by stealing her handkerchief. Thereafter, as soon as he came near attractive females, with violent sexual excitement, palpitation of the heart,
erection and *impetus coeundi,* the impulse would seize him to crowd up
against them and *faute de mieux,* steal their handkerchiefs. Although
the consciousness of his criminal act never left him for a moment, he
was unable to resist the impulse. During the act he was uneasy, which
was in part due to his inordinate sexual impulse, and partly to the fear
of detection.

Krafft-Ebing reported that, more than ten years later, this person was arrested again. Krafft-Ebing presents a case report of this second incident as described by a Dr. Fritsch of Vienna.

On searching his house, 446 ladies' handkerchiefs were found. He stated that he had already burned two bundles of them. In the course of the examination, it was further shown that X had been punished with imprisonment for fourteen days in 1883 for stealing twenty-seven handkerchiefs, and again with imprisonment for three weeks in 1886 for a similar crime. Concerning his relatives, nothing more could be learned than that his father was subject to congestions and that a brother's daughter was an imbecile and constitutionally neuropathic. X had married in 1879, and embarked in an independent business, and in 1881 he made an assignment. Soon after that his wife, who could not live with him, and with whom he did not perform his marital duty (denied by X), demanded a divorce. Thereafter he lived as assistant baker to his brother. He complained bitterly of an impulse for ladies' handkerchiefs, but when an opportunity offered, unfortunately, he could not resist it. In the act he experienced a feeling of delight, and felt as if someone were forcing him to it. Sometimes he could restrain himself, but when the lady was pleasing to him he yielded to the first impulse. He would be wet with sweat, partly from fear of detection, and partly on account of the impulse to perform the act. He said he had been sexually excited by the sight of handkerchiefs belonging to women since puberty. He could not recall the exact circumstances of this fetishistic association. The sexual excitement occasioned by the sight of a lady with a handkerchief hanging out of her pocket had constantly increased. This had repeatedly caused erection, but never ejaculation. After his twenty-first year, he said, he had inclination to normal sexual indulgence, and had coitus without difficulty without ideas of handkerchiefs. With increasing fetishism, the appropriation of handkerchiefs had afforded him much more satisfaction than coitus. The appropriation of the handkerchief of a lady attractive to him was the same as intercourse with her would have been. In the act he had true orgasm.

If he could not gain possession of the handkerchief he desired, he would become painfully excited, tremble and sweat all over. He kept separate the handkerchiefs of ladies particularly pleasing to him, and revelled in the sight of them, taking great pleasure in it. The odour of them also gave him great delight, though he states that it was really the odour peculiar to the linen, and not the perfume, which excited him sensually. He had masturbated but very seldom.

X complained of no physical ailments except occasional headache and vertigo. He greatly regretted his misfortune, his abnormal impulse — the evil spirit that impelled him to such criminal acts. He has but one wish; that someone might help him. Objectively there were mild neurasthenic symptoms anomalies of the distribution of blood, and unequal pupils.

When the winner of the 1981 World Series of Poker was asked what he planned to do with the money that he had won, he replied, "Lose it."[4] His remark reveals something about a class of varied and distinct psychiatric disorders which frequently take individuals afoul of the law but which receive relatively little attention in discussions of mental illness and responsibility. A salesman who exposes himself to female passers-by in the subway; a secretary who habitually shoplifts worthless trinkets; a father who inexplicably gambles away his family's savings; a man who makes sexual advances to his six-year-old niece: what these types of disorders have in common is, for lack of a better term, an aberrant desire — desires that most of us simply do not have. And for this reason, most of us never have to face the choice whether to yield. As Berlin puts it, "The average man does not refrain from having sex with five-year-old children or with eighty-five-year old adults simply because to act in such a fashion would be in conflict with his personal moral convictions. Rather, most men do not feel any substantial degree of erotic attraction to persons in those age ranges."[5]

In practice, we rarely excuse these individuals for their behavior. Typically, in fact, we hold them fully morally responsible. On the other hand, however, judging the responsibility of these people is not as simple as it is often portrayed. In ordinary circumstances, how we should judge moral responsibility is often intuitively clear, because we have ourselves been in similar circumstances. When we have not — and needless to say, with disorders like necrophilia or pyromania, this is probably usually the case — judging moral responsibility can be especially troubling.

These sorts of problems are often medically distinct, and may have little in common other than a desire that brings a person into conflict with prevailing moral standards or the law. They include some psychosexual disorders, such as pedophilia, voyeurism, exhibitionism, and frotteurism, as well as impulse control disorders, such as kleptomania, pyromania, and pathological gambling. (They might also include the obsessive-compulsive disorder, even though the disorder is itself quite distinct from the others and would not typically involve compulsions to act wrongfully or illegally.) What binds these disorders together is not just the fact that they involve desires that most of us do not have but that the person himself often does not want to have them. For want of a better term, I will refer to these types of problems as "volitional disorders."

It is probably safe to say that neither moral philosophy nor the law has found a satisfactory way of dealing with the volitionally disordered offender. Frequently, philosophical discussions of the problem become mired in irresolvable debates about psychological determinism or weakness of will. In this chapter, I will propose a way of morally characterizing the volitionally disordered offender that attempts to bypass (rather than solve) some of these problems. I will suggest that in at least some cases (but not all), we have good reason to exonerate the volitionally disordered offender from blame for his actions, and I will lay out a way of distinguishing those cases from those where the offender should be blamed. The analysis that I will outline is based on a broader moral category into which these individuals fall, that of necessity or duress.

Strength of Desire and the Irresistible Impulse

In Krafft-Ebing's case history, described above, the courts decided not to punish X for his offenses. The first court found that because of his "congenital mental enfeeblement" and "the pernicious influence of masturbation," X was *unable to resist* his pathological desire. The second court pardoned X on the grounds that he had "committed his crimes in obedience to an abnormal, irresistible impulse."[6] This reasoning converges with that proposed by many other people who have tried to argue for excusing the volitionally disordered offender, and who have centered their arguments on the strength of the offender's desire to act: the so-called "irresistible impulse" test.

Krafft-Ebing was himself sympathetic to the irresistible impulse test. He warned that the law should not hold individuals responsible for crimes committed as a result of "neuropathic" and "psychopathic" states. "Law is, in this, opposed to medicine, and is constantly in danger of passing judgement on individuals who, in the light of science, are not responsible for their acts."[7] Krafft-Ebing thought that a sexual offender should be excused, first, if he had lost any "moral or legal notions" to oppose the sexual desire; second, if the sexual desire was so intense that it clouded the offender's consciousness; and third, if the sexual desire was perverse and "intensified so as to be irresistible." Krafft-Ebing agreed with the courts that X's desire was irresistible, and for that reason he agreed that X should be exonerated. X's behavior resulted from an irresistible impulse to steal the handkerchiefs, and his impulse to steal resulted from his handkerchief fetish, which Krafft-Ebing called a "psychopathic state."[8]

On the irresistible impulse test, an offender is excused only when his desires were so strong that he could not help acting on them. That is, if a person could not prevent himself from acting, he should not be held responsible for the action. On the other hand, if it was in his power not to act as he did, then he ought to be held responsible for acting, barring any other excusing conditions or justifications.

This argument sounds reasonable enough. But it is important to realize that on the basis of the "irresistible impulse" test, the courts could have easily reached, on equally plausible grounds, just the opposite decision about X — that he ought to have been punished for his offenses. The reason is precisely the problem with the irresistible impulse test: for an observer, such as a court or a physician, it is difficult, perhaps impossible, to determine if the offender's desire was irresistible. Simply because the offender has acted on a desire does not mean that he could not have prevented himself from acting. Merely because a person *has* acted on a desire does not mean that he *had to* act on that desire. Who is to say whether a person did or did not have enough strength of will to prevent himself from giving in to his desires? The question is difficult enough to answer for the person whose responsibility is in question, much less someone else.

Nonetheless, there has been no shortage of attempts to answer it. One approach to determining whether an impulse is irresistible bases responsibility on the openness of the agent to persuasion. Glover, for example, argues that a person should be excused from responsibility for acting if his intention to act was unalterable — if he could not have changed that intention . But how do we tell when an agent's intention to act was unalterable? An intention is unalterable when the agent "is not open to being persuaded by reasons to alter it."[9] According to Glover, these reasons must be ones that the agent *himself* accepts as sufficiently good to make him change his mind if he were able to, or that he *would accept* as sufficient if he were able to reason properly.[10]

As an example, Glover offers the alcoholic. A nonalcoholic, temperate drinker might be persuaded to change his intention to have another drink before going home from a party, perhaps with a reminder that he is driving. However, says Glover, an alcoholic is not open to the same type of persuasion, because he cannot control himself in the same way — even if he accepts the reasons proposed as sufficient to change his mind. "The test of self-control, which differentiates my intention from that of the alcoholic, is that my intention can be altered by providing a sufficiently strong motive, while his can only be altered, if at all, by some form of manipulation such as behavior therapy or drugs."[11]

This last sentence hints at a practical difficulty with accounts such as the one Glover proposes. A desire that is irresistible under some circumstances will be resistible under others. In the case of Glover's alcoholic, it may well be that despite our most sophisticated arguments, he still intends to have another drink. Yet if I were to threaten him with a butcher knife when he insists on another, he might change his mind. Nearly any desire is resistible under certain circumstances, and any account of irresistibility must be adjusted to fit the particular circumstances under which the desire was not resisted.

What is more, even if an agent has deliberated, reached an all-things-considered better judgment, and then acted contrary to that judgment, this does not necessarily mean that he has done everything in his power to avoid acting.[12] As Mele notes, there is more to resisting a desire than mere deliberation, and a person can do any number of things to motivate himself to act in accordance with his better judgment. A voyeur whose desires were becoming difficult to resist might have concentrated instead on the problems that he would be causing for himself in the future. He might have placed a quick call to his wife, promised himself a reward for resisting, or, like Ulysses with the sirens, avoided the entire scenario with a little foresight. In the light of strategies such as these, the criteria for determining when an intention is unalterable become much more demanding.

The main problem, though, is familiar from philosophical accounts of *akrasia,* or weakness of will. The fact that a person judges that he has good and sufficient reason *not* to act in a certain way does not mean that, if he still intends to act, his intention to act is unalterable. It only means that it is irrational. And this is not just the case with the sick, the disordered, or the addicted. Suppose a married man spending the weekend alone is visited by an attractive neighbor, who begins to make seductive overtures. After a quick mental survey of his situation, the man decides that because of his moral duty to his wife, the high probability that she will discover that a sexual liaison has taken place, the potential psychological trauma to his children, and a medical condition that he fears will be exacerbated by such an encounter, it is best that he resist her advances. He then takes off his clothes, follows her to the bedroom and happily succumbs to temptation.

What are we to make of this action? Irrational? Certainly: the man has acted in clear opposition to what he has judged best. But his intention to act was not necessarily unalterable. With a bit more strength of will, he could have refrained from acting — or so we could well imagine. And this seems true not only for ordinary cases of weakness of will but also for paraphilias, pyromania, kleptomania, and so on. If we insist that whenever a person acts in opposition to what he has deemed best his intention to act was unalterable, then it becomes very difficult to distinguish between actions that are compelled and those that are simply irrational or stupid.

Of course, the problem of trying to guess whether a desire is truly irresistible becomes even more complicated with the volitionally disordered offender. As we have seen, estimating whether a desire was irresistible is a complicated task even when the desire is one's own. It becomes even more difficult when one must estimate the desires of someone else, and almost hopelessly perplexing when one must estimate the strength of desires that one does not even share.

The Quality of Desire

Given the problems of the irresistible impulse test, it is not surprising that some people have given up on the idea of desires that are irresistible. Joel Feinberg argues that for every case where a person gives in to a desire, "it will be true that if the person had tried harder, he would have resisted successfully."[13] If we want to assess the responsibility of individuals with volitional disorders, argues Feinberg, we need to look not at the strength of these desires but at their quality.

Consider exhibitionism, for example. Characteristically, the exhibitionist exposes his genitalia to unwitting strangers to achieve sexual excitement. Very rarely, however, does he attempt any actual sexual activity with these strangers. It might be an exaggeration to say that exhibitionists are *compelled,* in the strict sense, to act as they do, but they generally feel some mounting tension before the act of exposure — tension that is followed by a feeling of excitement and exhilaration after the deed.[14] Exhibitionism, Feinberg contends, is representative of a number of disorders, among which he numbers pedophilia, kleptomania, and fetishism, which are qualitatively distinguishable from ordinary desires.

First, says Feinberg, the "sick" offender's motives are characteristically unintelligible. While we can understand why a banker might embezzle funds or why a jilted husband might shoot his wife's lover, we are mystified as to why a person would want to expose his genitals to a stranger or feel a sexual attraction to footwear. Feinberg expresses this bewilderment nicely when he writes, "Here the old maxim 'to understand all is to forgive all' is turned on its ear. It seems closer to the truth to say of mentally ill wrongdoers that to forgive all is to despair of understanding."[15] The mentally ill offender's motives are unintelligible, claims Feinberg, because they are irrational: irrational in the sense that they are not self-interested; they fail to promote the offender's own good or well-being.

Now, the misdeeds of ordinary offenders are certainly not always for personal gain. Some people act wrongfully out of vengeance, others to advance an ideology. Yet as Feinberg points out, the wrongs of "sick" offenders do not seem to be "interested" at all — not self-interested, not other-interested and not cause-interested. In fact, they often seem to be completely contrary to the offender's interests. When the exhibitionist exposes himself, he might achieve immediate relief, but he gets no deep or lasting satisfaction.

Secondly, Feinberg contends that the motives of mentally ill wrongdoers are qualitatively distinct in that they are incoherent. "Their motives do not seem to fit together and make a coherent whole because one kind of desire, conspicuous as a sore thumb, keeps getting in the way."[16] The "ill" desires of the exhibitionist, the fetishist, the kleptomaniac or the pedophile are not integrated into his mental economy in the same way that his other desires are.

Finally and most important, "sick" offenders have very little insight into their own motives. Feinberg suggests that while an ordinary person realizes why he finds some actions appealing and others not, the reason a "sick" wrong-doer's action appeals to him is a matter about which he is fundamentally ignorant. The illness of the offender keeps him blind as to the true nature of his action's appeal. Feinberg suggests that this blindness is a "necessary condition of the illness itself."[17]

How, though, do these characteristics excuse the offender from responsibility? Feinberg's insights point toward the psychological complexity of the volitional disorders. But it is not at all clear that the characteristics he identifies are relevant to culpability. In fact, it is not clear that they are even unique to the mentally ill offender.

Feinberg argues that the actions of the mentally ill offender are unintelligible, and this because they are irrational. But surely this is not unique to crimes resulting from mental disorders. Vandalism seems senseless, does little to advance the vandal's interests, and often involves great risks to the vandal, yet we do not usually feel inclined to excuse him from accountability. Some might say that the vandal is mentally ill as well, of course, but here the distinction between crime and illness becomes uncomfortably fuzzy. Most of us are unwilling to excuse a criminal simply because we do not share his motivation.

Equally questionable is Feinberg's argument that the mentally ill offender's desires are in fact incoherent. Feinberg claims that the desires of the ill offender do not cohere because, unintegrated with the rest of the agent's desires, the aberrant desire keeps gumming up the works. But one plausible reason why this desire keeps gumming up the works is that it cannot be fulfilled. What is more, because the desire is seen as shameful or evil or both, it must be kept secret. If these desires could (somewhat implausibly) be fulfilled and openly acknowledged, there seems to be no reason to think that they would be any less coherent than our own.[18]

Feinberg also exaggerates the significance of the "sick" offender's lack of insight into his motives. Whatever insight the sick offender may lack is surely matched by that lacking in the rest of us. The ordinary person has little more insight into why he does *not* find handkerchiefs sexually exciting than Krafft-Ebing's fetishist has into why he *does*. Furthermore, we are all capable of acting irrationally without really knowing why. We act self-destructively, hurt the people that we love the most, and are often miserable at the times when we should be the happiest. As much as some of us would prefer to believe that we are models of rational thought, I fear that self-reflection often yields quite the opposite reaction — wonder at one's capacity for keeping the sources of one's beliefs and desires hidden. Feinberg himself recognizes this, in fact, and concedes that "even a person who is a model of mental health will often be ignorant about the *ultimate* basis of appeal in the things that appeal to him."[19]

Most important, though, even if the distinctions that Feinberg draws hold up, they do not give us any more grounds for saying that these offenders should not be held *responsible* for what they have done. It is not obvious just what it is about unintelligible, incoherent motives, about which the offender has little insight, that makes the offender any less responsible for his offenses. Feinberg's observations leave us more enlightened as to the offender's motivation, but not as to his culpability.

Compulsion and Duress

People with volitional disorders do not seem to be in a strict sense *compelled* to act, at least not characteristically. They can usually prevent themselves from acting as they do. But they are often in the position of having to choose between alternatives that, for one reason or another, are aversive or unpleasant for them. While choosing one bad alternative to avoid another is not as persuasive an excuse as many other excuses might be, we generally recognize that it is enough, at least in some cases, to mitigate the offender's blame.

It is sometimes said that when a person acts solely to avoid an especially terrifying alternative, such as a painful death, we cannot really say that avoiding that option is a free choice. Brodeur, for instance, says that these sorts of actions are "necessitated," and that I am acting under necessity when "a threat *compels me to choose* between alternatives which are all markedly repugnant to me and about which I never wanted to make a decision in the first place."[20]

But while it would be misleading to say that a choice between undesirable alternatives was a "free choice," equally misleading is to say that such actions are compelled. Being compelled to *choose* is one thing, being compelled to *act* another. Situations where a person must choose between aversive or undesirable alternatives are typically called cases of "necessity" or "duress." What is important for these cases is the fact that neither option is desirable. As McCall puts it: "What distinguishes duress from action that is perfectly 'free,' therefore, is the fact that in acting under duress we act contrary to our desires; what distinguishes duress from compulsion is that in compulsion we have no choice."[21]

In duress, unlike compulsion, there is at least some element of decision; a choice between Scylla and Charybdis is unfortunate, but it is still a choice. Indeed, these are the makings of tragedy: a figure faced with a choice between two terrible alternatives, either of which can be chosen only with great regret. It is precisely the fact that Agamemnon *chose* to kill Iphigenia that makes his choice a tragic one.

Duress is characteristically a choice between undesirables.[22] In cases of duress, one must typically make a choice between, on the one hand, doing a wrongful or otherwise undesirable action, and on the other hand, incurring some harm or evil. The person who has acted under duress typically has made the choice to act wrongly as a means of avoiding this harm.[23] Furthermore, the person under duress typically would strongly prefer not to be faced with the choice he must make. As an example, Aristotle cites the crew of a ship in a storm, who must throw goods overboard to secure the ship's safety.

Duress can be used as either an excuse or a justification. A justification typically concedes that the agent performed the action, but claims that the action is morally acceptable, while an excuse concedes that the action was morally wrong but challenges the agent's accountability for the action. In cases of duress, a person could defend his actions in either of these ways. In cases where it is offered as an excuse, an offender might say that because of the extraordinary circumstances in which he was placed, he made a bad decision. Tension, anxiety, the speed at which he had to make the choice — something about his situation contributed to his making a poor choice, and therefore he should not be judged so harshly. On the other hand, when the offender under duress claims a justification, he is saying that because of the undesirable alternative to his action, the action was morally defensible — that he was justified, or at least partially so, in acting as he did. (I will assume that if a volitionally disordered offender were to plead duress, he would most likely be offering it as a justification — claiming that his action should not be judged so harshly, because of the harm to himself that he was trying to avoid.)

Justifiable Action and Duress

If duress, used as a justification, depends on avoiding an alternative that is undesirable, then what counts as duress will differ from one person to the next. This is because what is undesirable will differ from one person to the next. If I hate my job, threatening to fire me will not be much of a threat; if I have a phobia for insects, the threat of being touched by one could be terrifying.[24]

Since duress typically involves a person who chooses a morally evil action as a way of avoiding harm to himself, it can be problematic in two ways. First, a person might not regard a so-called "harm," such as the loss of a hated job, as undesirable. Second, if a person has no moral scruples about the alternative, that alternative will probably not be undesirable either. Thus, the typical case of duress assumes that a person under duress who chooses to act wrongfully did not *want* to act wrongfully, but that he did so to avoid the alternative. Of course, it is often difficult to say how much suffering a person should undergo to resist causing someone else to suffer, but still, there is usually *some* point at which we would admit that acting in this way is morally justifiable.

Volitional Disorders and Duress

If the distinguishing feature of duress is a choice between undesirable alternatives, then the actions of the volitionally disordered will often qualify. They
will qualify in cases where the person is faced with the choice between (1) acting on desires that he finds morally repellent and shameful, and (2) refraining,
which causes him considerable distress.

There is reason to think that, at least in some cases, resisting these aberrant desires is much more unpleasant than resisting ordinary desires, because
of the considerable psychological distress that the person undergoes when he
resists them. In addition to the anxiety and discomfort that accompany resisting any strong desire, some people with certain volitional disorders undergo a process of mounting tension and anxiety until the action is carried
out. In the impulse-control disorders, for example, this escalating tension is
a diagnostic requirement for the disorder.[25] (It is worth remarking that these
disorders are quite rare, and the diagnostic requirements for pyromania, kleptomania, and pathological gambling will exclude the vast majority of fire-set-
ters, shoplifters, and gamblers.) Also well-documented are the anxiety and
dread felt by the person with obsessive-compulsive disorder who resists his
desires.[26] A similar process seems to occur in some psychosexual disorders.[27]
That these aberrant desires are very difficult to resist is also suggested by the
lengths to which volitionally disordered individuals will often go to satisfy
their desires — financial ruin, criminal prosecution, and the alienation of family and friends.

Krafft-Ebing's case history demonstrates these points vividly. His patient seems less a criminal than a pathetic figure in the grip of sexual desires
that even he finds strangely repellent. If it is not clear that his desires are irresistible, it is clear that they are very difficult to resist. His "uneasiness" and
"sweating" when he stole the handkerchiefs, the fact that he would "become
painfully excited, tremble and sweat all over" when he could not steal them,
the pleasure he got from the act, his personal testimony about the strength of
his desires, and the 446 handkerchiefs in his room: these aspects of X's case
suggest that his desires were very strong, and that he became very distressed
when he resisted them.

Also important is the fact that, as with more typical cases of duress, the
volitionally disordered person would often strongly prefer not to be faced with
the choice he must make. He has desires that he wishes he did not have, and he
is in a situation in which he would prefer not to be. Yet he must choose whether
to act on his desires or to resist. Krafft-Ebing's patient is a case in point; we
are told that X was remorseful, that he regretted his actions and "he had but
one wish — that someone might help him."

Now, several potential problems arise for a characterization of the actions of volitionally disordered agents as actions performed under duress. The first and most obvious is the need to ensure that the agent truly had to choose between undesirables. If a pedophile has no scruples about acting on his desires to molest children sexually, then he will have no guilt or shame about doing so and his action will not be an "undesirable" one. On the other hand, if he does not suffer any significant psychological distress (tension, anxiety, etc.) in resisting the desire, then this alternative is not an undesirable one either.

Second, we will also need some way to judge what actions are justifiable under what circumstances of duress. Criminal law, for example, traditionally excludes some offenses from being considered for a plea of duress: British law excludes murder, and Canadian law excludes murder, attempted murder, piracy, sexual assault, arson, and a host of other evils.[28] Aristotle gave matricide as an example of an offense that was not justifiable even under duress.

However, excluding some offenses from a plea of duress in the legal sphere does not necessarily mean that we should exclude these offenses from a plea of duress in moral matters. A primary consideration for the law is to deter people from acting criminally by punishing them. One reason for excluding murder as an offense for which duress can be pleaded is to deter people from choosing to murder when they are under duress.

But moral blame does not necessarily act as a deterrent, because, except for guilt or the disapproval of others, moral blame does not generally carry a punishment. So even if the prospect of legal punishment would deter a person under duress from choosing to commit an offense (and it is not entirely obvious that it would), it is very questionable whether the prospect of moral blame would do the same. Since deterrence seems to be the primary reason for excluding an offense from a plea of duress, it seems unlikely that there is any offense that we should automatically exclude.

The American Law Institute Model Penal Code handles the difficulty of deciding what actions are justifiable under what circumstances by appealing to the balance of evils incurred with each alternative action. It says that "conduct which the actor believes to be necessary to avoid an evil to himself or to another is justifiable, provided that the evil sought to be avoided by such conduct is greater than that sought to be prevented by the law defining the offense charged."[29]

Weighing the evils suffered with each alternative is a reasonable way to proceed with these sorts of judgment, but two qualifiers need to mentioned. First, even if we judge that the evils avoided by acting do not completely *justify* an action, we may still judge that the blame that we want to attribute to the agent should be *lessened.* We may judge that a person acted wrongly, but that the harsh circumstances under which he acted make him less blameworthy than he would be otherwise. On the other hand, some offenses may be so objectionable that only under extremely rare circumstances would we consider them justified. That is, we may not consider some actions by the volitionally disordered — pedophilia, for example — to be morally justifiable even if we were convinced that the agent was under duress.

Second, weighing one evil against the other in the way that the A.L.I. Model Penal Code suggests is not always a simple task, because we often believe that an evil suffered is not equal to an evil caused. That is, many of us would say that a person ought to tolerate harm to himself rather than permit harm to befall someone else — say, to suffer a broken arm rather than break another person's arm. (Though it sounds contradictory, perhaps we often *expect* people to act heroically.) However, this need not destroy the A.L.I. system. We might disagree as to where the fulcrum should be placed in this system of balancing evils to oneself and to others, yet still agree that the overall system of balancing evils is a useful one.

Finally, as we noted earlier, duress can be used as either a justification or an excuse, and the volitionally disordered offender might claim either of these. More commonly, he would argue that he was justified, at least to some degree, in acting as he did, because of the psychological distress he underwent in continually resisting his aberrant desires. "I did a terrible thing," he might say, "but I did it only because of the pain that I suffer when I do not do it." It is important to realize here that the agent is not claiming that he is not *responsible* for what he has done. He is fully responsible for his action. He is merely saying that under the circumstances, what he has done (and is responsible for) should not be seen as morally objectionable.

Less commonly, but in some cases equally plausibly, the volitionally disordered offender might claim an excuse. He might claim that although he acted wrongly, he should be excused (or his blame should be mitigated) because of the psychological stress he was under when he acted. In fact, in extreme cases of this sort, such as a state of panic, a person might be excused from responsibility not so much because of duress but rather because he was *compelled* to act. If a person is so overcome by fear that he is able to think of only one course of action (including that of not acting), then he might reasonably argue that his action was compelled. And if he was truly compelled to act — if he could not prevent himself from acting — then we should excuse him from responsibility for his action.

Problems

Some people might object that the predicament of the volitionally disordered is not one of duress, but rather one of temptation. We all face situations in which we are tempted to act on our desires, but when we do so and act badly, we could not legitimately claim to have acted under duress. Why should things be any different for the volitionally disordered?

The situations are indeed similar. And in fact we recognize this in our ordinary moral judgments about a person facing temptation. Because we can understand what a person must be experiencing when he is being tempted, we do not usually blame him to the full if he succumbs to the temptation. We recognize that it can often take extraordinary strength of will to resist.

Unlike temptation, however, the notion of duress is bound up with the idea of harm. Whether a situation counts as duress depends on whether he is somehow harmed both by choosing to act on a desire and by choosing to refrain from acting. The fact that many volitionally disordered offenders seem to experience such anxiety and distress when they resist, and such shame and guilt when they give in, suggests that unlike situations of ordinary temptation, they are faced with a choice between harms. There is also a case to be made that the person under duress is harmed in some sense by the mere fact of being in the situation. If a person's situation forces him to struggle with a choice, the process of which we believe to be itself very agonizing, we tend to be much more forgiving of his choice, no matter what it turns out to be. We realize that the person under duress would much prefer not to be forced to make the choice at all.

Also, the volitionally disordered offender differs from the person facing temptation in that he often has a second-order desire not to have his aberrant desires. A person tempted toward financial impropriety does not typically have a desire not to have a desire for money, and a person tempted toward marital infidelity does not typically have a desire not to have sexual desire. They may wish that they did not have such strong desires at those particular times, but generally they do not want to rid themselves of their desires altogether. Yet a kleptomaniac or an exhibitionist often seems to wish desperately that he could be completely rid of his aberrant desires.

A second objection to characterizing the volitionally disordered offender as acting under duress might be that, morally, one ought not to have desires such as these. But clearly, this objection is hard to sustain. First, why ought one not have such desires? The answer that the desires are "abnormal" will not suffice, because it leaves open the question of why one ought not to be abnormal. One could argue that such desires are wrong because they lead to dilemmas such as the one described, where others might be harmed. But this does not demonstrate that the desire is wrong in itself, only that it might lead to other harms. One could say the same of any desire. The relevant question with the volitionally disordered offender seems to be not whether one ought to have the desire but rather whether one could prevent having it.

Finally, one might object that for duress to apply, the source of duress must be external to the agent, and that with the volitionally disordered, the source is somehow internal. On a superficial level, there seems to be no reason why this must be true. For example, if a person were to act wrongly because to act rightly would aggravate a delicate medical condition, it seems reasonable to consider this duress even though its source was "internal." However, the source of this objection may be a more fundamental charge: that unlike ordinary cases of duress, with the volitionally disordered, the source of the duress is, in some sense, part of the person. These aberrant desires are an expression of the personality, and therefore the person who has them is somehow responsible for their existence.

This challenge is at its heart a version of objections familiar from debates over psychological determinism, and there is probably little that can be said here to contribute to a dispute so well-rehearsed. Nonetheless, several points about the particular predicament of the volitionally disordered person bear mentioning, if only briefly.

First, part of this objection stems from the suspicion that volitional disorders are more properly seen as part of the person's character than as "diseases," which are more easily seen as intrusions imposed onto the self from outside (and thus more like more ordinary sources of duress). Although we should exercise caution in appropriating behavioral aberrations for inclusion under the medical umbrella, the disorders of volition resemble more typical "diseases" in several important ways, and thus may be at least more like diseases than like facets of the individual's character. First, like most diseases, and unlike some other psychiatric problems such as the personality disorders, these volitional disorders are often unwanted by the person who has them. Second, as with many diseases, the volitionally disordered person generally did not cause his condition. Third, like most diseases, without treatment the person cannot rid himself of his condition. (It might also be worth mentioning that the obsessive-compulsive disorder often responds to medication.) Finally, as with many diseases, the person suffering from a volitional disorder often himself sees his condition as intrusive and alien, not as something that is an essential part of his "self."

Second, it should be noted that in presenting duress as a way of characterizing the volitionally disordered offender, I have not suggested that the offender's psychological condition *determined* his actions. I have only suggested that given his peculiar situation, which seems to be markedly different from that of most of us, he seems to have more *justification* in acting as he does than we might normally think, and that we should lessen his blame accordingly.

Criminal Law

Although my concern has been mainly with moral and not legal responsibility, a few comments on legal responsibility may be helpful here, since the sorts of offender with which this chapter has been concerned are generally held legally responsible for their actions. I have argued that we should exonerate (or at least lessen the moral blame that we place on) many volitionally disordered offenders. However, moral exoneration plainly does not necessarily entail legal exoneration. In deciding whether a person is legally blameworthy and thus punishable, we take into account not only moral blame and justice but also considerations of utility: protection of innocent victims, deterrence of other potential offenders, deterrence of the offender himself, and so on. One could argue (though it would be a difficult argument to make) that for these reasons we should hold the volitionally disordered offender legally responsible and punish him for his wrongs, even if we are convinced that he is morally blameless.

These considerations notwithstanding, two points must be kept in mind. First, to argue that we should punish the morally blameless to deter them from acting similarly in the future would require strong evidence that punishment will, in fact, deter them. However, in many sorts of volitional disorder (psychosexual disorders, for example), there seems to be little evidence that punishment is an effective deterrent.[30] A much more effective way of changing many offenders' behavior seems to be psychiatric treatment. For this reason, treatment will also be a more effective way of protecting potential victims.

Second, when we argue that the threat of punishment is necessary to deter *potential* offenders, we must remember that there are very few potential offenders to deter. Most persons have no desire whatsoever to expose themselves to strangers, say, or to steal worthless trinkets. The argument for deterring potential offenders is strongest when we have reason to believe that a much larger number of people would commit the offense if the offense were not legally punishable. It is weakest when, even if it were not punishable, only very few people would commit the offense.

Case History

By way of conclusion, it might be helpful to examine a case history reported in the *Canadian Medical Association Journal* concerning a 25-year-old man who sought treatment for his exhibitionism at the clinic of a psychiatric hospital after a series of arrests for indecent exposure.[31] The man would frequently disrobe and hide in a wooded area near the center of the town where he lived, then expose himself to women who passed by. Occasionally, after entertaining fantasies of exposure, he would stop his car on a side street and expose; he would also often hide in the cloakroom of a girls' school and expose himself to students. The authors note:

> The attack of exhibitionism was described by the patient as being preceded by a feeling of sexual excitement and dread. He would experience a "grim determination to expose, come what might." He would become tense and an erection would occur. At this time things would seem unreal, "as if watching myself in a dream." He would then expose himself to the female usually but not always masturbating. When the girl registered shock, "the spell would be broken," and he would flee, trembling and remorseful.[32]

The patient had begun exposing himself at the age of thirteen and continued throughout his adolescence. When he was fifteen, he began to make lewd telephone calls as a substitute for exposing when exposing was not possible. After this, there followed a period of voyeurism. The authors state, "By the late teens and early twenties, his exhibitionism had reached bizarre proportions. Tension was constant and it was not unusual for him to expose several times a day."[33]

By the time he contacted the clinic, the patient had been arrested for indecent exposure twenty-four times. On twelve occasions, he had been convicted, with nine prison sentences varying in length from four months to one year. He had been treated for his problem with psychotherapy, but without success.

During one period, the patient arranged to have a prosthetics manufacturer construct for him a "chastity belt" so that he could prevent himself from exhibiting. His wife would lock the belt in the morning and unlock it at night. However, the patient was arrested for indecent assault while wearing the belt, for attempting to grasp the breasts and legs of a woman he saw in a crowd.

Two features of this case are noteworthy. First, during the times when the patient was not exposing himself, he was in a constant state of tension, and his urge to expose became much stronger in certain situations. Resisting his desires was plainly a highly distressing effort. Second, it is clear that the patient wanted very much to rid himself of his desires. He sought treatment and was apparently cooperative, and when he exposed himself he felt remorseful. As with Ulysses' command that he be bound to the mast, the patient even went so far as to wear a chastity belt, anticipating that his will would become weaker in the future.

It seems clear that this man was facing a situation of duress. Both resisting the desires and giving in to them were aversive to him; resisting brought on a state of tension and distress, and giving in brought shame and remorse. To avoid even being in the agonizing situation of having to choose, he sought psychiatric treatment. The criminal law obviously was not successful in dealing with this man. Twenty-four arrests and nine prison sentences had not done much to stop him from exposing himself. Questions of justice aside, pragmatic considerations suggest that psychiatric treatment would be a better alternative than prison.

Conclusion

I have argued that duress is a helpful way of morally characterizing the situation of a certain type of psychiatrically disordered offender. However, while this characterization is a useful way of framing the moral argument, two caveats are clearly in order if it is to be put into place. First, whether duress will apply to a given offender will hinge on whether that offender has suffered psychological distress, and this distress cannot be assessed for a group in a blanket fashion. It will vary from one disorder to the next, from one person to the next for a given disorder, and from one time to the next for a given person. Second, duress is contingent on the agent's having only alternatives that are aversive. Psychiatric treatment may be another alternative to acting on a given desire, and if an offender has consistently and knowingly avoided treatment, then the plea of duress will not apply.

Bearing these cautions in mind, however, it seems clear that we should consider the actions of many volitionally disordered offenders as actions performed under duress. In some cases, of course, the balance of evils suffered and caused may not convince us that the offender should be exonerated. Pedophilia would be one common example; another would be macabre paraphilias that, in rare cases, lead to even more serious crimes.[34]

In other cases, however, such as exhibitionism, where the harm caused seems to be minimal and the harm incurred by resisting seems substantial, it seems reasonable to exonerate some offenders, or at least to lessen their moral blame. If the plea of duress is valid for a volitionally disordered offender, then we are obligated to consider him less blameworthy for his moral wrongs.

The next chapter turns to a much larger class of psychiatric problems, the personality disorders. As with the "volitional disorders" discussed in this chapter, conventional moral thinking generally holds people with personality disorders fully morally responsible for their actions. In contrast to the arguments in this chapter, however, I will argue that conventional moral thinking is right: that it is justifiable to hold people with personality disorders fully accountable for what they do.

4

Character Judgments and the Personality Disorders

"Mad or bad?" goes an old (and by now rather hackneyed) question: was he ill, or simply evil? The reason for asking the question, of course, has always been its weighty implications for moral responsibility. If a person is sick, then presumably she cannot be held responsible for her actions; if she is well, she can. Madness, it is affirmed, precludes badness.

That so many psychiatric diagnoses have moral connotations should make us think carefully before assuming that madness and badness are, as asking this question implies, mutually exclusive. Designating a person a pedophile, a sadomasochist, a psychopath or a narcissistic personality is not exactly a value-free undertaking. It suggests, rather, that a person can be both mad and bad, and to suspect one does not necessarily rule out the other.

The aim of this chapter is to show how judgments of moral responsibility are related to judgments of character, and thereby to judgments of badness and madness. I want to argue that, contrary to the arguments of some, judging that a person is morally responsible for an action is conceptually distinct from judging that he is evil, or judging that he is mentally ill. To say that a person is *responsible* for an evil action is not to say that he is sinful or vicious (though that may also be the case); it is to say that he deserves the moral credit for the action, in this case the blame. More importantly, though, if we say that a mentally ill person is *not* responsible for an action, this is not because mentally ill people are not bad people (though, again, that may often also be the case) but because the mental illness affected the person's thinking in some relevant way.

The tangled connections between assessments of moral responsibility, judgments about moral character, and diagnoses of mental disorders are best illustrated in patients with personality disorders. The personality disorders test, in an especially acute way, our intuitions about character and responsibility. In what follows, I will try to unpack some of those intuitions by suggesting that judgments of responsibility are essentially judgments about a connection between agent and action, and that these types of judgments must be distinguished from questions about a person's character.

Case History

Gene Brown was a 29-year-old textile factory worker who came to a university psychiatric clinic because he had been sexually impotent with his wife for approximately eight months. The impotence began several weeks after he had begun working on another shift at the factory; as a consequence he now worked the same shift that his wife worked, and was at home during the same time of the day as she. During the previous three years, when he had worked on another shift, he had pursued extramarital affairs with a number of women, and now his shift change had made these liaisons much more difficult to arrange. He found these new arrangements upsetting, and on several occasions he had attempted unsuccessfully to convince his employer to change his schedule again. He was not impotent with any woman other than his wife. He admitted to physically abusing his wife on occasion; this had happened more frequently in recent months and on several occasions had resulted in visits to the hospital emergency room.

Mr. Brown had grown up in rural Texas and had lived there for most of his life. His father was alcoholic, and was often away from home for long periods of time. When Mr. Brown was six years old his mother had died. From the age of six until the age of nine he had lived with an aunt and uncle, from whose home he was removed by the state for reasons of neglect. Later he had lived in various foster homes. His father had abused him during his early years; Mr. Brown recalled being burned with cigarettes and being held under water while he was supposedly being taught to swim.

Mr. Brown was a very large, physically imposing man who spent a great deal of his time at body-building exercises. He stood about 6'4", weighed 280 lbs. and usually wore tight sports shirts that highlighted his muscular build.

Mr. Brown often arrived late for his appointments at the psychiatric clinic, and when he did he usually demanded to be seen immediately. He seemed surprised and angry when he was told that he would have to wait. He also expected his medication to be given to him free of charge. His manner was condescending and self-important; he usually made a point of telling his psychiatrists a joke or a story that reflected his contempt for doctors, especially psychiatrists. He spoke constantly of himself and his accomplishments — his athletic talents, his financial skill, and especially his attractiveness to women. He once boasted that he had slept with fourteen women in one night, and he discussed his extramarital affairs with some pride. He said that before his shift change he was sleeping with seven women regularly, one for each night of the week. His physical strength was also a favorite topic, and he recalled with amusement a number of violent confrontations in which he had bested his co-workers. His short temper seemed to be the cause of several of these incidents. He openly discussed his past altercations with his wife, which frequently erupted after his episodes of impotence. He claimed that his impotence was her fault. Despite having broken her nose and arm in their past disputes, he expressed no sympathy for his wife or remorse for his actions. He stated that she should consider herself fortunate that he had married her, since he could have married any number of women who were more attractive. He also expressed suspicion that she was having an extramarital affair.

After several visits to the psychiatric clinic, it also emerged that Mr. Brown had a fear of using public lavatories. This fear had bothered him for nearly ten years, but it had not presented many problems recently because the factory where he worked had single lavatories, which could be used by only one person at a time.

Personality Disorders

Cases like this one can be especially troubling for an account of moral responsibility, because they tug at our intuitions from two opposite directions. On the one hand, the man's background of abuse and neglect as a child may incline us to say that he cannot really be blamed for what he has done. He seems as much an appropriate object of pity as of blame. On the other hand, everything he has done has been done intentionally, even maliciously, and without remorse: his abuse of his wife, his marital infidelity, and his dishonesty. Surely this is a paradigm case of morally bad behavior.

In addition to his social phobia and his sexual impotence, the patient in the preceding case would probably be diagnosed by many American psychiatrists as having the narcissistic personality disorder. Patients with personality disorders often have none of the problems that we are most apt to call mental "illness" — no delusions or hallucinations, no compulsions or phobias. What patients with personality disorders have are character traits that cause them or others problems of some sort, often problems in social relationships. The DSM–IV criteria for the narcissistic personality disorder include a sense of self-importance, a pattern of grandiosity in behavior or in fantasy, a lack of empathy, and a sense of entitlement.

Though the personality disorders comprise recognized diagnostic categories in both ICD–9–CM and DSM–IV, it is a term that to some psychiatrists — in the words of some recent commentators — "lacks respectability."[1] One reason for this lack of respectability probably stems from questions about the therapeutic usefulness of the concept. But another reason probably stems from questions about what it is, conceptually, for a personality to be disordered. It seems plain enough that some people have character traits that prevent them from living full and fulfilling lives; what is more controversial is whether these character traits are best understood as psychiatric problems.

Nonetheless, for a variety of reasons patients with these sorts of character traits often come to the attention of psychiatrists. Psychiatry generally regards these problems as deserving of psychiatric attention if they cause the person subjective distress or, perhaps more controversially, if they impair the person's ability to function in society. DSM–IV and ICD–10 offer broadly similar definitions of personality disorders; both focus on the longstanding nature of personality traits and their ill effects on the individual.

ICD–10 defines the personality disorders as "deeply ingrained and enduring behavior patterns" which usually begin in adolescence and persist throughout most of adult life. Personality disorders manifest themselves as "inflexible responses to a broad range of personal and social situations."[2] ICD–10 adds that because of this deviation, "the disorder leads to considerable personal distress, but this may only become apparent late in its course."[3] DSM–IV concentrates on impairment in social and interpersonal functioning. It says that the essential feature of personality disorders is an "enduring pattern of inner experience and behavior that deviates markedly from the expectations of the individual's culture," manifesting itself in at least two of four areas: cognition, affectivity, interpersonal functioning, or impulse control. It also stipulates that this pattern must be inflexible and pervasive across a wide range of personal and social situations, and that it must lead to "significant distress or impairment in social, occupational or other areas of functioning."[4]

There is broad agreement that, at least to some extent, personality disorders can be classified into various types. There is less agreement as to what those types are. For example, both DSM–IV and ICD–10 recognize and describe in similar ways the paranoid and histrionic personality disorders, but DSM–IV has no equivalent for the ICD–10 masochistic personality disorder.

Other diagnostic categories overlap, but do not correspond precisely. ICD–9–CM lists the explosive personality disorder, which DSM–IV does not list; however, DSM–IV does include the intermittent explosive disorder as one of the impulse control disorders. These variations should not be too surprising. It seems reasonable to assume that personality traits exist on a spectrum, present or absent in degrees about which there will not always be agreement, and that these traits can be associated to a greater or lesser extent both with other personality traits and with other psychiatric disorders.[5]

Whatever the difficulties of diagnosing and treating persons with personality disorders, it should be plain that some persons have character traits that cause them or others problems of one sort or another, and that these persons occasionally — even frequently — act in ways that many of us feel justified in morally criticizing. The question at hand concerns the nature of that criticism: how do judgments that a person is psychiatrically disordered or that he is evil relate to judgments about whether he is morally responsible for his actions?

Madness or Badness

The introduction to this chapter implied that the classification of "mad or bad" was a misguided way of framing the issue of moral responsibility and mental illness. It is misguided because of the way that it inclines us to think about questions of responsibility: specifically, that when we excuse a mentally disordered person from responsibility for her actions, we do it because madness precludes badness. A person who is sick is not morally responsible for her actions, the question implies, because sick people are not evil.

The pervasiveness of this picture of illness and responsibility should not be underestimated. It can be seen in most public debate on criminal responsibility, which usually gets no further than caricature: conservatives accusing liberals of seeing all socially deviant behavior as illness, to be treated rather than punished; liberals accusing conservatives of glossing over the injustice of punishing the mentally ill. The antipsychiatry movement that came into vogue in the 1960s and 1970s played on the widespread feeling that psychiatry was overstepping its bounds — that psychiatrists saw every unpleasant aspect of social life as potentially pathological. In rebellion, the antipsychiatrists took an ideological leap in just the opposite direction, claiming that mental illness was a myth, and really little more than a means of social control.[6]

Underlying much of this debate is a misunderstanding about just why we exonerate the mentally ill for their actions. That misunderstanding is that we exonerate the mentally ill simply *because* they are mentally ill. If that is in fact the case — if we do excuse people from responsibility simply because of a diagnosis of mental illness — then the fear that psychiatrists see all problems of character and behavior as psychopathological suddenly seems much more reasonable. A moral scheme that excuses people from responsibility for their actions solely because they are mentally ill is profoundly threatened by a psychiatric scheme that greatly broadens the scope of pathology. If socially deviant behavior and bad character automatically count as psychopathology, and psychopathology automatically counts as an excuse, then there seems no limit to what sort of behavior can be excused.

One of the most well-known early critics of psychiatric overreaching was Lady Wootton, who asserted that the psychopath "is, par excellence, and without shame or qualification, the model of the circular process by which mental abnormality is inferred from anti-social behavior, while anti-social behavior is explained by mental abnormality."[7] What Lady Wootton seems bothered by here is the notion that bad behavior is seen as evidence that a person is mentally ill, the fact of which is in turn used as way to excuse that person from responsibility for the behavior. However, the process to which Lady Wootton objected is not a circular one if we do not allow mental disorder *per se* as an excuse. There is nothing wrong with inferring a medical condition from a symptom and then using that condition to explain the symptom. For instance, one might infer from the facts that a person is continually thirsty and urinates frequently the hypothesis that he has diabetes mellitus, and the diabetes would then be an explanation of the symptoms.

Where we go wrong is in using antisocial behavior or bad character to diagnose "mental disorder" (e.g., a personality disorder), and then using the mental disorder as an *excuse* for the antisocial behavior. But here it is not the claim that anti-social behavior is a sign of mental disorder which is unjustified, but rather the further claim that mental disorder is itself an excuse from responsibility for antisocial behavior.

Even so, some caution is called for here. The idea that the personality disorders are illnesses should give us pause. First, when the diagnosis of an illness is made, it is usually for the purpose of treatment, be it cure, control or palliation. For personality disorders there is often no effective treatment. Second, for many (but not all) illnesses there is (or there is suspected to be) an underlying organic, physiological abnormality. For most personality disorders there appears to be none. Third, most illnesses are unwanted, and this could not be said of many personality disorders. Finally, most medical diagnoses are not made *solely* on the basis of behavioral signs, as the case is with most personality disorders.[8]

Mental Illness, Vice, and Excusing Conditions

If the reason that we exonerate mentally ill people from responsibility for their actions is the bare fact that they are mentally ill, then obviously quite a lot depends on what counts as mental illness. But ordinarily this is not the case. Ordinarily we exonerate the mentally ill from responsibility for their actions not simply because they are mentally ill but because of the particular way in which their disorders have affected their thinking. If we exonerate an exhibitionist for exposing himself, it is not simply because he is "mentally ill" (which may in fact be a debatable point), but because he had strange desires that caused him such distress to resist. And if we exonerate a psychotic person with paranoid delusions for attacking his mother, it will ordinarily be not simply because he is mentally ill but because (for example) he had the delusion that he was acting in self-defense. What matters here is not so much what we call mental illness as the particular ways in which a disorder affects the way a person thinks about his actions.

Nevertheless, the idea that what is important is mental illness itself has its philosophical defenders. By this account, the individuals whom we should exonerate are those whose actions reflect or manifest the fact that they are mentally ill. The reason we should exonerate them is that if they are mentally ill, they are not evil, because mental illness is distinct from bad character.

While this position might sound reasonable on the surface, it leads to some conclusions that are difficult to accept, especially for the personality disorders. Yet because the argument is so superficially plausible — and, to judge by public debate, apparently so widely held — it is worth looking at in some detail.

One of the more sophisticated variations on this position comes from Robert Cummins, who argues that the reason that we exculpate mentally disordered persons is that their actions are not characteristic of a vice. Ordinarily when we exculpate a person, Cummins says, we are saying that "the commission of the offense does not reflect ill on or tend to morally discredit the agent."[9] On the other hand, when we blame an agent for an action, we do it by establishing that the action is fully characteristic of some vice. Cummins states:

> An act is characteristic of a vice if it is the sort of act which standardly manifests it, as stuffing oneself standardly manifests gluttony, and lying standardly manifests mendacity. An act is *fully* characteristic of a vice if it is characteristic of that vice, and actually a manifestation of it. Thus bravado may be a manifestation of cowardice, but is not characteristic of it, and lying, though characteristic of mendacity, may, on some occasions manifest a virtue and hence not be fully characteristic of mendacity.[10]

Thus, says Cummins, when we ask whether an agent should be exculpated, we are asking if the agent's offense is "fully characteristic of the sort of relatively permanent trait that we call a vice or permanent defect, i.e. a trait that is appropriately assessed morally."[11]

To see how the mentally disordered are exonerated from responsibility, says Cummins, consider the case of a man on a deserted beach who spots a child being swept out to sea in a raft. Though he is a former swimming champion, the man is paralyzed by a phobia of water. Instead of plunging in after the child, he watches as the raft disappears. Cummins asks: what distinguishes this phobic from a coward? The actions, or lack of action, of the coward and the phobic are both characteristic manifestations of some longstanding character trait. The distinction, Cummins claims, is that a phobia is not a vice in the same way that cowardice is.

However, Cummins says, we should realize that mental illness is not an *excuse* from responsibility, in the same way that ignorance or compulsion might be. Rather, mental illness "exculpates" because "mental disorders are not moral defects, i.e. not proper subjects of moral assessment."[12] In other words, the inaction of the phobic is indicative of a character trait, but a trait that also happens to be a mental disorder, and the phobic is not blameworthy because mental disorders are not the sort of character traits about which we can make moral judgments. Unlike the morally evil, the mentally ill do not have morally flawed characters.

Fields puts forward a similar argument, contending that the reason that we exculpate the mentally ill person is that his actions do not indicate a "morally bad attitude." Like Cummins, Fields argues that when we exonerate a mentally ill person, it is because we have concluded that his action does not reflect badly on his character. When we *blame* offenders, on the other hand, we do it because "we regard a person's action or omission as a sign or manifestation of an attitude which he has, and which we judge to be a morally bad attitude."[13]

For example, if a paranoid man has the delusion that his neighbor is an enemy agent intent on murdering him, and as a consequence he assaults the neighbor, all the while believing that he is acting in self-defense, he should be exonerated, because his "attitude is not morally defective." A malicious hoodlum might perform the same action simply to flatter his own vanity, and this would indicate a "morally vicious" attitude. But the paranoid man, according to Fields, shows no such malevolence. The same goes for a voyeur. "If a person's voyeurism is truly compulsive," Fields contends, "we are prepared to excuse him, for in such cases the agent's behavior does not manifest a blatant disregard of, or contempt for, the tender feelings of loving couples and their wish not to be spied on."[14]

Character and Moral Credit

The flaw of models such as those that Cummins and Fields put forward is their reliance on a faulty picture. This picture locates judgments of responsibility *within* judgments of character. It says that when we assess responsibility, we are really making a moral judgment about a person. My argument, in contrast, is that judgments of moral responsibility are judgments not about character but about *credit* — whether a person deserves the moral credit, the praise, or the blame, for an action.

Both Cummins and Fields assume that when we make judgments of responsibility, we are judging the doer, not the deed, and not the connection between the two. Fields claims, for example, that with our judgments concerning blame, our moral disapproval is directed at a *person* rather than at an action or omission. "Moral blame, then, is an attitude of moral disapproval towards a person for doing what one oughtn't, in general, to do."[15] Cummins is more direct. "It is offenders, not conduct, which we must incarcerate or treat or blame, and our behavior is rational only insofar as it fits with what we can discover about offenders from their conduct."[16]

The underlying assumptions here are that in judgments of responsibility for actions, we look at an agent's behavior as a symptom of an underlying disease of character, and that we are interested in the behavior only for what it tells us about the person. This assumption, however, is fundamentally mistaken. When we judge responsibility for actions, we attempt to decide what the person *deserves,* not what he is like. Our decision is about whether the moral weight that the action carries belongs in the hands of the agent. Now, when we decide this, we may of course discover things that will mold or alter our moral opinion of the agent. But this is not what the judgment of responsibility is essentially about; it is an accompanying feature.

When we look at a person's character, we are judging personality traits that are, by their nature, relatively longstanding — a person's attitudes and behavior over time. Judgments of responsibility, in contrast, are one-shot affairs. They are judgments about single actions, about the connection on a given occasion between a person and an event.

Thus, when we judge whether or not a person should be held responsible for an action, it does not matter whether she has a vice, a bad character, or a bad attitude; the question is whether she deserves the moral credit for the action. The question of whether a person is good or evil is different from that of whether he was responsible for an action. Good people can do, and be responsible for, bad things. In contrast, by stipulating, as Cummins does, that for an agent to be culpable for an action that action must be "fully characteristic of a vice," we rest moral responsibility on the supposition that we can fault only repeat offenders, those people with a *disposition* toward committing the offense. But this is not how judgments of responsibility work. When we say that a person is morally responsible for an action, we are not saying anything about her disposition toward performing these sorts of actions or about whether she has performed these sorts of actions in the past. We are simply saying that she deserves the moral credit for this single action.

Suppose, for example, that someone insults me. Do I excuse him if I find that he has never done this sort of thing before, or that he has no disposition toward this sort of behavior? Of course not. I will consider him responsible for the offense — never mind if he possesses a vice of which his behavior is fully characteristic. If I am sure that at all times save this one he is a model of civility and manners, I may think more of him as a person; I may make more of an effort to understand this uncharacteristic lapse; I may well be more willing to forgive and forget — but if he performed the action knowingly and freely, I will still hold him morally responsible for this one-time aberration. On the other hand, if I discover that his insult was a misunderstanding, that he did not *intend* to insult me, I will *not* hold him responsible, even if I find that he ordinarily insults people simply for amusement. What he has done in a particular case and what it is his habit to do are different matters entirely.

This brings us to a second problem. While judgments of character are often (but not always) judgments concerning the moral goodness or badness of a given trait or disposition, judgments of responsibility are not, in themselves, judgments of moral goodness or badness. Questions of responsibility are questions about a *connection*. When we ask whether a person is morally responsible for an action, we are asking whether there is a link between that person and the action. Of course, we will also be interested in whether the action was morally good or bad, but that question is not about whether the person was responsible; it is about what sort of action the person is responsible for.

To make this point is to say no more than that morally good people can intentionally do evil things, and that morally evil people can intentionally do good things. The fact that a person has a morally good or bad character does not affect our judgment of whether he is responsible for a given action. For that matter, neither do questions about the morality of actions. Judgments of responsibility hinge on whether the action was done freely, knowingly, intentionally, and so on — and these questions are independent of the morality of the action or of the character of the person who performed it.

Of course, things are not always so simple. Concepts such as "blame" blur the lines between judgments of character and judgments of responsibility, because to say that a person should be blamed for an action also implicitly reflects ill on that person's character. Having a bad character is connected, in complicated ways, to doing bad things. But this connection does not alter the basic distinction between judgments of responsibility and judgments of character.

Personality and Responsibility

When we are able to conceptualize mental disorders as illnesses, as a type of glitch in a person's brain function, then we generally find it easier to consider the mental disorder as an external entity imposed upon the victim's character, and consequently as something that has no bearing on our moral assessment of her character. On the other hand, with many of the problems that come to the attention of a psychiatrist, such as the personality disorders, we are inclined to think of the disorder as somehow *part* of a person's character — or at least not so clearly separable from it. This point is well illustrated in the case history described at the start of the chapter. With the personality disorders, it is difficult to conceptualize the person's character flaws and his psychiatric problems as independent entities.

As the personality disorders demonstrate, it is difficult to base a claim for exonerating the psychiatrically disordered on whether the person has a morally bad attitude, because a morally bad attitude is itself often a symptom of the disorder. It would be hard to claim, for example, that the person with the antisocial personality disorder does not have a morally bad attitude when the diagnostic markers of his condition include such a litany of moral breaches: lying, cruelty to animals and people as a child, failure to respond to family responsibilities, irritability, aggressiveness, failure to honor financial obligations — not to mention an absence of remorse about any of this behavior.

Nor are the difficulties of distinguishing between a morally bad attitude and a mental disorder limited to the personality disorders. Take, for instance, the case that Fields describes, a person with paranoid delusions. If a person is hostile, suspicious, and argumentative, as a person with paranoid schizophrenia might well be, it is difficult to argue that he does not have a morally bad attitude, or that his delusion-inspired actions are not indicative of that attitude.

It hardly needs saying that we ordinarily consider people with personality disorders morally responsible for their actions. Those of us who know people with disagreeable character traits are rarely inclined to excuse them, even if these traits are so disagreeable as to make them anxious or unhappy. And the diagnosis of personality disorder usually does little to persuade psychiatrists that these persons are not responsible for the unpleasantness they cause.[17] The reason should be fairly obvious: when persons with personality disorders act badly, they are usually thinking clearly and acting intentionally.

Nevertheless, cases like these are troubling. If a person's action results, at least in some weak sense, from his character, and if his character is a product of conditions largely outside his control, then to hold him responsible for that action seems unjust.

This feeling does not, of course, hold only for the personality disorders, or even for mental disorders as a whole. We are troubled by this difficulty when we encounter *most* cases of wrongdoing. A person's character is determined largely by his upbringing and his genetic inheritance, factors outside his control. And as commentators on psychological determinism have repeatedly pointed out, it seems unjust to hold a person responsible for something that is outside his control.

Now, it would be wrong to argue that we command what sort of characters we have. We are not completely powerless in this respect, of course; there is some sense in which, as Aristotle maintained, we make our characters by our actions. But even the most optimistic of us will confess that we exert only limited control over our personalities. Nevertheless, this powerlessness is not why we feel that holding people responsible for their characters is *unjust.* If we are all powerless in this respect, at least we are all *equally* powerless. In the degree to which we are helpless in the face of unsympathetic nature, there is, if nothing else, parity.

Rather, our feeling of injustice comes from the fact that nature is often unkind. It seems unjust to hold a person responsible for his character when nature is so capricious in how she distributes her wealth. When the circumstances of one person seem to make it so much more *difficult* for him than it is for others to be morally good, then it seems unfair to hold him morally responsible for his wrong actions to the same degree that we hold a person whose circumstances have been more fortunate.

Given, then, this unfortunate situation, where some of us are endowed by our circumstances with much more than others, how do we preserve some sense of fairness and consistency? A world with no system of moral responsibility is inconceivable. If we had no way of connecting the moral import of actions to persons, we would have no morality. The very idea of an action's being morally good or bad, as opposed to merely having fortunate or unfortunate consequences, depends on there being a person who did the action. So the question with which we are left is how to make *more just* a system of moral responsibility which seems to be intrinsically *unjust.*

We ordinarily respond to this problem naturally by focusing our system of responsibility around those things that, unlike his character, a person does have some control over — whether he did the action intentionally, how he acted if he was under duress, whether he acted recklessly or negligently, and so on. While the framework in which a person sees and deliberates over his actions

— his beliefs, desires, values, and so on — will be largely out of his control, we hold him responsible as much as we can only for how he acts *within* that framework, rather than for the framework itself.

Still, we are left with the problem of how to respond to the offender of obviously flawed character, whose defects are clearly not of his own doing, but who nonetheless intentionally acts badly. How can we blame, for example, the child abuser who was himself abused as a child? The difficulties here for cases of psychiatric disorders are particularly acute. In many problematic psychiatric cases, no delusion or compulsion affects how the agent thinks about his action; rather, the patient has longstanding neurotic problems that are resistant to treatment, and that color his thinking in much more subtle ways.

However, we should remember that there are many nuances to our system of responsibility. We do not simply either hold a person responsible for an action or exonerate her; we can hold a person morally but not legally responsible, blame her but not punish her, or, perhaps most important of all, blame her but forgive her. However, the thread that holds the whole system together is the connection between action and agent. This connection we base on a person's *intention:* her knowledge of what she was doing, her willingness to do it, and so on. A person's upbringing and genetic inheritance are immaterial to the question of whether, in a given situation, she *intended* to act. So, if we want to mold our system of responsibility to correct some of the injustices of nature, we should do it, if possible, in a way that affects *least* this thread that links an action's moral import to its agent.

We can take the injustices of nature into account in many ways, such as by refraining from punishing those we blame, or by forgiving them. But deciding to forgive, or not to punish, does not mean deciding that a person is not morally responsible. Rather, they have to do with the way we deal with a person *after* we have judged him to be morally responsible. By handling in this way the circumstances that formed a person's character, we are able to leave intact the tenuous connection between action and agent which lies at the foundation of a system of moral responsibility.

Conclusion

To make a judgment about the responsibility of the mentally ill for their actions is not to make a judgment about the content of their characters but, rather, to make a judgment about the connection between agent and action. A person's mental illness may well affect that connection, and it may affect her character, but judgments about all these things are conceptually distinct.

The fact that a person has been diagnosed with a personality disorder should not ordinarily be reason to exonerate that person from responsibility for her actions, in the absence of any other excusing conditions or mitigating factors.[18] A person with a personality disorder who behaves badly ordinarily *intends* to behave badly, and people should generally be held accountable for what they have intended to do. We might want to be more forgiving toward such people, and more sympathetic toward their plight, but this does not mean that we should not hold them responsible.

The next chapter, however, concerns a particular type of personality which might well be an exception: the psychopath. The psychopath is exceptional because of the peculiar character of his deficiencies, which, it has often been said, include an inability to understand moral concerns. If this is in fact the case, if the psychopath is unable to understand morality, then it would seem unjust to blame him for acting immorally. However, just what it means to understand morality — and to fail to understand it — are not entirely clear. Chapter 5 takes on these questions in detail, and concludes with the suggestion that in some cases, the psychopath's blame for his wrongdoings should be mitigated.

5

Morals, Lions, and Psychopaths

Psychopaths are a problem.[1] They are a problem for the courts, which do not know whether to punish them; for their families, who do not know whether to trust them; for neuropsychiatric researchers, who do not know what is wrong with them; and for psychiatrists, who do not know how to treat them, or even what to call them. As a result, they are an intriguing problem for philosophers, raising all manner of intertwined conceptual questions about moral knowledge and responsibility.

In a nutshell, the problem of the psychopath is one of understanding: not of facts but of morality. When the psychopath acts badly (as he often does), does he know that what he is doing is wrong? Is he as sane as he often appears to be, or is his apparent sanity merely a mask, concealing deficiencies that should exonerate him from responsibility for his acts? The answer is even more elusive than it might initially seem, because the psychopath's deficiencies are notoriously difficult to pinpoint. Plainly, he is deficient is some way, and in some way related to morality. But just how the psychopath's deficiencies are related to morality raises vexed questions about what it means to understand morality and how much understanding is necessary for moral responsibility.

This chapter will address the question of whether the psychopath understands morality. While there are difficulties in answering that question of any person, it is especially difficult to answer in the case of the psychopath because of his unusual and controversial deficiencies. I want to suggest that, while the psychopath's deficiencies preclude a full, conceptually rich understanding of morality, the psychopath is capable of enough moral understanding to be held accountable, at least in a limited sense, for some of his actions. It is helpful to

71

begin by exploring just what the psychopath's deficiencies are. Many of these are illustrated in the following case history, taken from Hervey Cleckley's classic work *The Mask of Sanity*.

Case History

Max was a white man in his forties who was brought to a veteran's hospital after he was arrested and convicted in South Carolina for check forgery. In the past he had been hospitalized in various psychiatric units for treatment of his mental disorders, and both his wife and VA officials argued that he was not responsible for his actions. For this reason, an agreement had been reached whereby he would receive psychiatric treatment rather than a prison sentence.

Physical examination on admission revealed a small man, alert and oriented, with no signs of psychosis or any other physical or mental disorder. A test for syphilis was positive, but a lumbar puncture showed no sign of neurological involvement. Engaging and clearly very intelligent, Max spoke proudly of his birth in Vienna, his many achievements in sports, and his scholarly work as a student at the University of Heidelberg. He said that at Heidelberg, Kant and Schopenhauer were his special objects of study, and he also mentioned his deep interest in Shakespeare. He spoke of his skill at fencing, remarking that he was well-known, even feared, in Heidelberg and Vienna for his deadly skill with the sword. He denied all the criminal offenses that had brought him to the hospital.

His medical records showed that he had been admitted to psychiatric hospitals on six previous occasions. During none of these admissions had a symptom of an orthodox psychiatric disorder been noted. On his last admission he had initially been friendly and cooperative with the hospital staff, but soon became disruptive in rather petty ways, such as encouraging fights between mildly psychotic patients.

Several months before that admission he had been admitted to a veteran's hospital in Maryland; he had complained of having blackout spells where he would lose his temper and unknowingly attack people. These spells were especially unfortunate for his victims, he claimed, because he had at one time been the featherweight boxing champion of England. He described seizures lasting up to ten hours, during which he would convulse so violently as to rattle the windows and shake the slats off his bed.

Records also showed that in the past Max had been convicted and fined on many occasions for minor frauds, forgeries, and street fights. He had usually escaped prosecution with the help and the apparently sincere concern of his wife, in spite of the fact that since marrying her, he had also undertaken two different bigamous marriages, all this in addition to another previous legal marriage which had ended in divorce. His present wife was the proprietress of a brothel, but even she appeared to be embarrassed by the behavior of her husband, who apparently intruded frequently upon the brothel's guests, insisting on reminiscing nostalgically about his sports achievements, often parading and roaring at the closed doors behind which the clients were conducting their business.

About two-thirds of Max's time appeared to be spent away from home, going from city to city and living by his wits — apparently living quite handsomely from the various ingenious illegal schemes that he had devised. He was also able to avoid much time in jail by convincing authorities that he was mentally incompetent as a result of a head injury he had sustained in the Army. After one such trip away, a quarrel with his wife erupted when Max brought one of his bigamous wives home to the brothel for a visit. This dispute escalated into a brawl and culminated in the brothel's near-destruction. Max also broke his legal wife's nose, for which eventually — after an additional series of check forgeries — he was arrested. But such were his gifts of persuasion that it was not long before his wife was won over again and began to reconsider. Soon she arranged for his admission to a psychiatric hospital instead of prison. This was the occasion of his present hospital admission.

On the ward, Max was very cooperative for a while, but soon became restless and hostile. On one occasion he kicked out an iron grill and escaped from the hospital, taking two psychotic patients with him. He committed petty thefts and started fights on the ward, and on the one occasion when he was granted leave from the hospital, he escaped from his attendant through a tiny bathroom window and made his way to the nearest bar.

When, at the request of his wife, he was moved to another ward, he became more agreeable, and began boasting that he was a gifted artist. On one occasion in the presence of his psychiatrist, he requested a loaf of bread. He then broke off a large chunk which he placed in his mouth, chewed, removed, and then modeled into a large crucifix, complete with pedestal, rosettes, and a garland of intertwining leaves. This mixture of bread and saliva hardened quickly, and in time Max began painting these crucifixes and presenting them to the staff.

Despite his seemingly odd behavior, Max was described by Cleckley as an exceptionally intelligent man. Cleckley thought that Max would easily have been able to earn an M.D. or a Ph.D. at most American universities. In the weeks following his admission, Max began to get in touch with local members of the community who were interested in welfare work and in helping disabled veterans. Soon these well-intentioned people began to bring pressure on the hospital to allow Max to rehabilitate himself. On several occasions he was given parole, but each time, sometimes after only a few hours, he would become involved in a fight and be brought back to the hospital by the police. He was eventually released from the hospital; two months later local newspapers began to carry reports of patched-up ten and twenty dollar bills circulating in several Texas cities. Federal agents soon traced these to Max, who had somehow devised a method of cutting up five bills and pasting them back together — only the result was not five bills but six, with no appreciable loss in size. Schemes like this continued over the following years, with Max usually escaping punishment by referring officials to his psychiatric history. On one occasion, he claimed amnesia; on another, he convinced authorities he was schizophrenic, by claiming that he could communicate with his dead ancestors. On a third, he convinced them that he was deluded, by claiming that he was being chased by baboons.

Moral Insanity and the Psychopath

What does this man deserve, the psychiatric ward or a jail cell? The patient, if we can call him that, shows many of the characteristics that have been attributed to psychopaths over the years: impulsive behavior, a lack of any enduring emotional attachments, disregard for the law, poor judgment, superficial charm, and intelligence. But more important, he shows evidence of what is certainly the most consistently described feature of the psychopath, and that is an inability to understand or appreciate moral concerns.

The origins of the present-day notion of psychopathy and its connection to moral understanding are often traced to J. C. Prichard's 1835 *Treatise on Insanity and Other Disorders Affecting the Mind,* in which Prichard introduced the diagnosis of "moral insanity" into English medical practice. At the time of Prichard's treatise, Franz Joseph Gall's writings on phrenology were widely influential, and it was thought that various human propensities could be localized anatomically in the brain. Moral insanity was believed to be a deficiency in the moral faculty, that part of the brain thought to be concerned with making choices between good and evil.[2]

Benjamin Rush, to whom Craft traces the origins of psychopathy, described a condition he called "moral depravity": "The moral faculty, conscience and sense of deity are sometimes totally deranged."[3] Rush believed that "there is probably an original defective organization of those parts of the body which are occupied by the moral faculties of the mind."[4] This characteristic deficiency in the "moral faculties" appears consistently, although in different guises, with other descriptions of the disorder. For example, the British Mental Deficiency Act of 1913 referred to the "moral imbecile," a term that was later amended to "moral defective" in the 1927 Mental Deficiency Act. The 1927 Act defined the disorder as "mental defectiveness coupled with strongly vicious or criminal propensities" and noted that moral defectives "require care, supervision and control for the protection of others."

Karl Jaspers' writings in 1923 indicate that the ancestor of the present-day "psychopathic" or "antisocial" personality disorder was taking shape by this time:

> They strike us as strange creatures, highly exceptional in many ways: their destructive drives are unaccompanied by any sensitivity for what is right, they are insensible to the love of family or friends, they show a natural cruelty alongside feelings that seem strange in the context (e.g. a love of flowers), they have no social impulses, dislike work, are indifferent to others' and their own future, enjoy crime as such and their self-assurance and belief in their own powers is unshakable.[5]

Probably the closest present-day equivalent of the psychopath in North America is the DSM–IV antisocial personality disorder. However, the antisocial personality disorder is defined primarily not in terms of personality traits but in terms of irresponsible and antisocial behavior, such as a lack of enduring emotional attachments or frequent brushes with the law.[6] As a result, the line is blurred between what many writers have called psychopaths and what other people call criminals. Nonetheless, the DSM–IV conditions for antisocial personality disorder include a "lack of remorse" for wrongdoing, a criterion that hints at the disorder's historical antecedents.

Two Characteristics of the Psychopath

For our purposes, two consistently described characteristics of the psychopath stand out. The first is what I will argue is the psychopath's defective moral understanding, variously described as an absence of conscience, a lack of moral sense, or an inability to feel guilt or remorse. The second characteristic, less often noted by philosophers but perhaps related to the first, is the psychopath's notoriously poor judgment.

The philosophical literature often portrays the psychopath as a cool, remorseless manipulator who, while impervious to the stings of conscience, is extraordinarily adept at achieving his own egoistic ends. In contrast, the figure of the psychopath that appears in psychiatry differs radically in at least one respect: this psychopath often acts in ways that are remarkably imprudent, even from his own perspective. Not only is this characteristic abundantly clear from the case history described above, it is one of the most consistently described features of the disorder. Jaspers remarks that the psychopath seem to be indifferent to his own future; Cleckley observes that he seems to follow no life plan;[7] and Gelder notes that he fails to learn from adverse experiences.[8] In fact, while the psychopath often seems pathologically egocentric, he is nothing like an enlightened egoist. His life is frequently distinguished by failed opportunities, wasted chances, and behavior which is astonishingly self-destructive. Cleckley is persuasive on this point, pointing to the familiar example of the psychopath who "in full possession of his rational faculties, has gone through the almost indescribably distasteful confinement of many months with delusional and disturbed psychiatric patients and, after fretting and counting the days until the time of his release, proceeds at once to get drunk and create disorder which he thoroughly understands will cause him to be returned without delay to the detested wards."[9]

The psychopath's consistently bad judgment suggests that his deficiencies are more complicated than they seem. In fact, pinning down just what these deficiencies involve is one key to unraveling the question of the psychopath's moral responsibility. However, answering the question of whether the psychopath understands morality is hindered by another formidable obstacle, that of psychiatric nomenclature. At various places and times since the early nineteenth century, psychopaths have also been known as sociopaths, antisocial personalities, asocial personalities, moral imbeciles, morally insane, and morally depraved. This would be a confusing but not an especially serious problem if these various names were attached to the same people. Unfortunately, however, with different titles come different shades of meaning, especially on different continents. Here, as in other areas, Britain and North America are separated by a common language. The British psychopath, it seems, is a very different species from his North American cousin. The case from Cleckley's book would be a prototypical psychopath in the North American literature, sometimes called the "primary psychopath": cool, glib, manipulative, and superficially charming. The British literature, on the other hand, more often portrays what are sometimes called "secondary psychopaths," usually described as highly anxious, withdrawn, tense, and socially inept. But both the primary and the secondary types are impulsive and seem to thrive on excitement, and both seem to lack ordinary moral inhibitions.[10]

Moral Ignorance and Moral Understanding

The crucial question for judgments of moral responsibility is whether the psychopath understands morality. As the M'Naghten Rules imply, it would be unjust to blame someone for acting wrongly if that person did not understand that what he was doing was morally wrong. But with many psychopaths, this question is obviously not so easy to answer. Even if the psychiatry of psychopaths were more straightforward, there is a philosophical problem about the concept of moral knowledge. Briefly put, the problem of saying whether the psychopath knows right and wrong is tied to the problem of trying to say, with any kind of certainty, what *is* right and what is wrong, when there is so much disagreement about it even among nonpsychopaths, such as philosophers. And if *we* cannot say with one voice what is right and wrong, then it is hard to say that the psychopath should be excused because *he* does not know it.

Nevertheless, philosophical arguments for and against excusing the psychopath can be found in abundance,[11] and most of the arguments for excusing the psychopath construe the psychopath's deficiencies as a sort of ignorance: ignorance of what makes an action morally wrong. Just as we would not hold a soldier responsible who unknowingly kills his sergeant, mistaking him for an enemy, we cannot hold the psychopath responsible for acting wrongly if he truly did not know that his action was wrong.

However, the comparison between ignorance of facts and ignorance of morality is not as straightforward as it might seem. Just as ignorance typically draws its force as an excusing condition by virtue of its relationship to the facts of a situation, ignorance of morality, if it is to be an excusing condition, will seemingly draw its force by virtue of a relationship to *moral* facts. However, even if moral facts exist — and of course, there is no consensus that they do — just what they are is something about which there is wide disagreement.[12] Since we will still want to hold ordinary, nonpsychopathic wrongdoers morally responsible for their actions, to exonerate the psychopath we must show that ordinary wrongdoers know what the moral facts of a situation are while psychopaths do not.[13] In the light of centuries of philosophical debate over moral knowledge, skepticism, and subjectivism, this is no easy task to accomplish.[14]

However, while it is difficult to construe the psychopath's deficiencies as ignorance of moral facts, it is pretty clear that there is something about morality, vague and undefined though it may be, which the psychopath does not know, and which the rest of us do know. This has been described with a fair amount of consistency since the mid-nineteenth century. The real question is not *whether or not* the psychopath knows; the real question is just what it is he does not know, and what it is he does.

What he does know is what other people think is wrong. He knows what most people feel guilty about, which actions will be punished, which will be rewarded, when to lie and when to tell the truth. In fact, he often knows all these things well enough to be able to manipulate, flatter, and bamboozle people with something approaching genius. The psychiatric literature is replete with tales of the guile and charm of many psychopaths, and the extraordinary exploits that often result.

On the other hand, the psychopath seems to lack any sort of deep engagement with morality. His knowledge seems limited to morality's most shallow and superficial features. This sort of deficiency can be difficult to describe, a bit like describing a person who is able to say in the most technically correct, clinical terms why Duke Ellington was the greatest jazz composer of the century, yet who is also clearly and unquestionably tone-deaf.

Hints at this sort of deficiency come through obliquely in most descriptions of the psychopath as an inability to feel remorse, guilt, or shame. Cleckley claims that although the psychopath's superficial charm and congenial manner may be deceptive, the psychopath "does not show the slightest evidence of humiliation or regret. . . . If Santayana is correct in saying that 'perhaps the true dignity in man is in the ability to despise himself,' the psychopath is without a means to acquire true dignity."[15]

More revealing, however, is a deficiency that Cleckley describes as a paucity of insight: the inability "to see himself as others see him."[16] Cleckley suggests that the essential defect in the psychopath is an utter inability to appreciate what gives meaning to other people's lives. This sometimes comes across as a sort of bizarre, paradoxical kind of *sincerity:* the words that the psychopath is using are invested with an emotional depth that he is totally unable to comprehend, and precisely for that reason, he is able to use them with complete earnestness. Cleckley remarks of one patient that he is "not so much a genius at acting but . . . a person who . . . has no capacity for distinguishing between what is acting and what is not."[17]

Cleckley's remarks suggest the real problem in trying to say whether the psychopath understands morality. The psychopath's deficiency is not so much in understanding "the moral rules" as in understanding the subtleties of morality — the interplay between moral concepts, the more nuanced aspects of moral language, how morality works as a social institution. It would be a stretch, for instance, to say that the psychopath truly understands the *importance* of morality. And any conception of morality that leaves out morality's importance will be incomplete; a morality that was trivial would not be recognizable to us as morality. Without an adequate conception of morality's importance, the psychopath would not fully understand why people believe moral commitments to be binding, or why moral concerns generally outweigh other concerns.

It seems plausible that the psychopath may also fail to grasp fully the idea that moral values are in some ways self-developed: that embracing a moral value involves more than blindly accepting what others say is morally right or wrong. A deep appreciation of morality implies an understanding of the process of examination, criticism, and modification which accompanies the acceptance or rejection of a moral value. It also implies an understanding of how a person's moral values are in some sense a part of that person, and how a person's character could be changed by acceptance of a moral value. A deep engagement with morality involves more than simply knowing what moral norms are; it also involves embracing them, endorsing them, making them one's own. It seems unlikely that a psychopath would have as rich an understanding as most of us of what it means to be unprincipled or insincere.

It is also worth remembering that the psychopath characteristically has an shallow emotional life. Of course, how (or whether) this will affect his understanding of morality will depend on how one sees the relationship between morality and the emotions, but it should be uncontroversial to say that a person with little capacity to feel emotional attachments will experience a void in an area which for most of us attaches very closely to our moral commitments. Could a psychopath really understand gratitude, for instance, or forgiveness, and why we think these things are important? Or the contrast between the detached, disinterested standpoint of a certain conception of morality, and the passionately interested standpoint of love? Probably not with the richness and intensity with which any ordinary person can.

This points toward the nub of the problem in trying to say whether the psychopath "understands the difference between right and wrong." Ordinarily, we can make, and sustain, sharp distinctions between knowledge and motivation: between knowing something and being motivated to do it. Moral emotions like guilt, shame, pride, gratitude, and embarrassment motivate most of us to do the right thing most of the time. Of course, sometimes we know that something is wrong and do it anyway; sometimes, we do not even feel guilty about it. But a lack of motivation and a lack of guilt do not mean that we do not know that what we have done is wrong. If this were all there were to the psychopath's deficiencies, then surely he characteristically knows that what he has done is wrong, and should not be excused.

What the case of the psychopath calls into question is the sharp, bright line between moral knowledge on the one hand and moral emotions and motivation on the other. For clearly, the psychopath is much more complicated than an ordinary person who simply feels no guilt or empathy. The fact that the psychopath shows deficiencies in both knowledge and motivation suggests that, at least in the case of morality, knowledge and motivation go together.

One line of thinking that might follow is that we cannot hold a person responsible for his moral transgressions if he does not understand morality, and that a person cannot understand morality without *caring* about morality. This seems to be the idea that Gilbert Ryle was getting at when he wrote:

> Here, too, there seems to be an incongruity in the idea of a person's know-
> ing that something wrong had been done, but still not approving of it or
> being ashamed of it; of his knowing that something would be the wrong
> thing for him to do, but still not scrupling to do it. We hanker to say that,
> if he has no scruples at all in doing the thing, then he cannot know that it
> is wrong, but only, perhaps, that it is 'wrong'; i.e. what other people call
> wrong.[18]

Ryle contends that just as it seems incongruous to speak of a person's knowing the difference between good and bad wine or good and bad poetry without caring more for one than the other, it is difficult to imagine a person who knows the difference between a good and a bad action without being concerned about it. This sort of understanding is similar to an educated taste. "Knowing, in this region, goes hand in hand with approving and disapproving, relishing and disrelishing, admiring and despising, pursuing and avoiding."[19]

On the other hand, while concern and knowledge may in general go hand in hand, it seems unlikely that concern is necessary for *all* sorts of moral understanding. For example, I may have an intimate knowledge of but little concern about the moral practices of the Zulus. Nor is the connection between knowing and (say) admiring or relishing as tight as Ryle avers. It is not entirely senseless to speak of admiring something for its badness (as Ryle acknowledges at the end of his essay). A kitsch aesthetic blurs distinctions between beauty and ugliness, and between admiring and despising — hence my enjoyment of a 1950 Japanese science-fiction film that I acknowledge to be terrible.

Nonetheless, Ryle is certainly right in saying that in questions about values, knowing and caring cannot be so easily separated. We can find clues of this connection in the psychopath's deficiencies. The fact that the psychopath does not seem properly to *understand* moral concerns is related to the fact that he seems to *have* no moral concerns. The psychopath does not seem to be able to see why the interests of others matter. This incapacity is especially crucial for morality, because ordinarily we expect that the interests of others must be important to a person *self-evidently*. To the question, "Why do the interests of others matter?," there seems to be no answer that would be convincing. One is inclined to give the same answer that Louis Armstrong gave when asked what makes good jazz: "Man, if you gotta ask, you'll never know."

Moral Imagination and the CNV

Given that there are at least two consistently described features of the psychopath — moral insensitivity on the one hand, and strikingly bad judgment on the other — the natural question to ask is whether or not these two features are related. Could there be any link between the two? It is tempting to imagine that the psychopath has some sort of defect in the imagination, some sort of cognitive defect that impairs his ability to see himself in other contexts: to see himself in the future, for example, or, perhaps even more important, to see himself in the position of another person. Could there be some sort of broad-ranging impairment that affects the psychopath's ability to incorporate complex information into the mental processes that go into these sorts of deliberation?

There is some extremely tentative but suggestive evidence for a conclusion like this in the work of Howard,[20] who has looked extensively at psychopath's EEGs — in particular, the Contingent Negative Variation, or CNV, a slow negative potential change that occurs in the cerebral cortex when a subject is preparing for a motor task or a mental task. The CNV measures anticipatory states — those states when a person is preparing to respond to a stimulus of some sort.

Howard has compared the CNVs of psychopaths and normal controls on a GO/NO GO paradigm. In the GO/NO GO paradigm, the subject has his EEG measured while he hears one of two different sounds. He first hears either a high-pitched sound or a low-pitched sound, which tells him he is in either the GO arm or the NO GO arm of the paradigm. With the high-pitched sound, in the GO arm, the sound indicates that in two seconds the subject will see a red flashing light, in response to which he should press a button. And if he hears the low-pitched sound, he knows that he is in the NO/GO arm, which means that in two seconds he will see a green flashing light, to which he should *not* press his button. If he responds incorrectly — if he pushes his button when the sound has told him not to, or if he does not push his button when the sound has told him he should — then he receives a punishment in the form of a loud noise.

What is interesting about Howard's findings is that, outwardly, there is no difference between the responses of psychopaths and normal controls. Both are equally able to tell which arm of the paradigm they are in and respond in the right way. But at the same time, they show conspicuous differences in their measured CNVs, the EEG measurement of their state of anticipation. The profiles of normal controls show that when they are in the GO arm of the paradigm and are preparing to respond, their profile shows a CNV or a large negative potential change; but in the NO GO arm, when they are *not* preparing to respond, they show very little or no CNV.

But the EEG profiles of primary psychopaths are different. They do not show these conspicuous differences between GO and NO GO conditions. Their EEG profiles look very similar, regardless of whether they are in the GO or the NO GO arm of the paradigm. In other words, whether the psychopath is outwardly anticipating an action, or outwardly *not* anticipating an action, his EEG shows very little change in *its* measurement of his state of anticipation. What does this suggest? Most interestingly for our purposes, it suggests that psychopaths differ physiologically from normal controls in the way that they anticipate their responses to future conditions. Making moral and prudential judgments beyond a certain level of sophistication requires attending to and filtering out a vast amount of complex information — information about future conditions, how they are likely to change, subtle emotional cues, nuances of manners and morals. It is possible that psychopaths have cognitive defects that bear on their ability to attend to and incorporate complex information into their intentions, perhaps even to imagine themselves in other contexts. It is tempting to speculate that psychopaths have a subtle cognitive impairment that affects both their moral and prudential judgment.[21]

Wittgenstein and Psychopaths

Part of my concern up to this point has been to point out that the psychopath shows deficiencies not only in his sensitivity to moral concerns but also in his prudential judgment, and in the shallowness of his emotional attachments. Another concern has been to argue that these deficiencies are connected: specifically, that understanding morality is in some way connected to caring about it. The question I would like to turn to now is whether there might be something absent from the psychopath's experience that impairs his ability to understand morality.

The later Wittgenstein was concerned to show that language, including our moral language, is not simply a self-standing way of representing the world, and that understanding what a word means is more than simply knowing what it stands for. Language, according to Wittgenstein, is part of an activity. It is part of an activity in that it is embedded in a wide scope of human practices, and to get at the meaning of a word, you have to understand how it is used in these practices. Clearly, to understand what the word "checkmate" means, you have to understand something about the game of chess — the rules of the game, the point of it, the fact that it is a game, and so on. Wittgenstein famously used the term language-game to highlight how speaking a language is part of an activity, or he says, of a form of life. Wittgenstein asks, for instance: "What would a society of all deaf men be like?" We could answer that obviously members of such a society would not have the ability to understand, in the same way that we do, the language that hearing people use to describe sounds. And they would probably have a somewhat different vocabulary for the practices by which they communicated instead of speaking: for example, if they used sign language instead of the spoken word, one could well imagine an entire vocabulary used to describe the way people moved their hands, in the same way that we have a very rich vocabulary to describe the tone and timbre of the human voice — shouting, singing, whispering, whining, drawling, shrieking, and so on.

Wittgenstein made the point even more strikingly in another well-known and characteristically cryptic aphorism: "If a lion could speak, we could not understand him."[22] The point he was getting at, of course, was that any language of which a lion might theoretically be capable would be embedded in a form of life so different from our own, with such vastly different concerns and practices and activities, that the lion's language would make no sense to us.

It does not seem too far-fetched to suggest that the psychopath is something like the lion; that the psychopath's deficiencies leave him incapable of fully participating in our form of life. By our form of life I mean, first, one which includes the rich and subtly complex ways in which people relate to each other emotionally — as friends, lovers, colleagues, confessors; and secondly, that includes the diversity of *moral* commitments that are interwoven with those relationships. Out of this form of life has emerged a very rich moral vocabulary, involving not only basic moral terms such as rights and duties but also thick ethical concepts such as cruelty, betrayal, honor, kindness, and so on. It may well be that to fully understand this vocabulary, you must be capable of experiencing the form of life out of which it emerges. And this is where the psychopath, with his moral and emotional poverty, falls short. Just as a deaf man will not be able to fully understand our vocabulary of sound, the psychopath may be incapable of fully understanding our vocabulary of emotion and morality.

Nonetheless, it would be a mistake to conclude that because the psychopath has no moral values himself, he has no understanding of the moral values of others. Duff takes this position, arguing that understanding requires "that we have moral values, and a moral language, of our own; *and* that we find logical connections between our concepts and others: we come to understand them by tracing out these connections."[23]

However, even if we were to concede that the psychopath has no moral values, and that this void precludes his understanding the moral values of others, this does not mean that the psychopath has *no* understanding of morality. It might preclude an understanding of why people regard morality as important, and of why people regard moral obligations to be binding, but it does not preclude an understanding of what these moral obligations *are*. That is, it may be that a person must value and care about certain ways of behaving to see *how* others value certain ways of behaving, or it may be that a person must approve and disapprove of some sorts of acts before he can see *how* others approve and disapprove of some sorts of acts. But surely this is not all there is to understanding. A person without these values could be capable of seeing *that* others value certain ways of behaving. Doubtless, this is understanding in a detached, intellectual sense, yet it does comprise some part of what it means to understand.

Conclusion

As for moral responsibility, this leaves us with a rather mixed conclusion. Because even if the psychopath is incapable of as rich and vivid an understanding of morality as most of us, he obviously still understands quite a lot — not unlike, perhaps, the sort of understanding an anthropologist might have of an alien culture that she can observe but not fully participate in. Is this limited understanding sufficient for moral responsibility?

Probably the best alternative is to regard psychopaths, in a moral sense, in much the same way that we regard adolescents. We blame them when they act badly, but we also recognize that they do not have the full moral appreciation of their actions that we would expect of adults. We blame adolescents or mitigate their blame according to their maturity and their understanding of what they have done. If it is clear that a psychopath understands to a certain minimal degree the moral import of his action — that others universally regard it as morally wrong, that others are blamed and punished when they do it — then we would obviously feel more justified in blaming the psychopath for the action, even if we do not blame him to the same degree that we would an ordinary adult. On the other hand, we should feel less justified in blaming a psychopath for actions that involve the subtleties of moral reasoning or emotional commitment — such as, for example, some questions of sexual morality.

The practical question of what to do with psychopaths is another question entirely, and at best, even more difficult. There is no answer that is entirely satisfactory. The problem with sending psychopaths to prison is, first, if psychopaths have some sort of diminished responsibility for their actions, it is not clear whether this severe a punishment is fair; second, at least some psychiatrists, such as Cleckley, believe that prison does not deter psychopaths from committing crimes again; and third, since psychopaths often commit relatively trivial crimes, sentences are usually not very long, and the result is simply a longstanding pattern of going in and out of jail. The problem with involuntary commitment to a psychiatric hospital, on the other hand, is that psychiatric treatment does not seem to do much good either. If a "cure" is the condition for release, then the psychopath may well stay locked up for a very long time. This may be justifiable when the patient is potentially violent, but it hardly seems a fair way to treat petty criminals.

Perhaps the only hopeful part of the psychopath's typical course is that the more outrageous behavior seems to diminish with age. A recent study found that fifty percent of patients with antisocial personality disorder met none of the criteria by age twenty-nine, and eighty percent met none of the criteria by age forty-five.[24] As for treatment options, we are left with little more than the recommendation by an expert committee set up in Australia in 1991 to study the antisocial personality disorder, which said that "there is no known specific treatment for this disorder," but that "a calm temperament is a great asset. . . ."[25]

The psychopath is a unique problem because his deficiencies are, first, so closely connected to criminal behavior, and, second, so closely connected to his character. The term "disease," as with the personality disorders as a whole, does not fit the psychopath's problems very well. By contrast, chapter 6 largely concerns problems that fit the disease model much more comfortably. The delusions that are often symptomatic of the psychotic disorders, such as schizophrenia and bipolar disorder, frequently influence questions of criminal responsibility in a very dramatic way. In some cases, they are the very paradigm for insanity as an excusing condition.

6

Beliefs, Delusions, and Identity

What we do is tied to what we believe. But the threads that tie our beliefs to our actions can be frustratingly difficult to untangle. Intertwined with our beliefs and actions are our intentions and motives, our desires and values, our hopes and worries and concerns. Untangling these threads is difficult enough in ordinary human beings, but in the often impenetrable world of the mentally disordered, it can become almost hopelessly complex.

Nevertheless, the ties between beliefs and responsibility are often crucially important to understanding the mentally disordered offender. This chapter is an effort toward untangling those ties, by examining several case histories, and by characterizing some of the more straightforward ways in which the psychiatrically disordered patient's beliefs may influence her moral responsibility for her actions. More controversially, I want to suggest that, in some cases, a person's personality may change so dramatically as a result of mental illness that we should regard her, at least from the standpoint of responsibility, as a different person.

Case History

Mr. MS was a 64-year-old man admitted for paranoid schizophrenia.[1] Born in eastern Poland, Mr. MS was a single, unskilled laborer with little formal education. He had joined the army at the age of seventeen, and when the USSR invaded Poland in 1939, the Soviets had imprisoned him and forced him to work at several labor camps. After his release, he was sent to the United Kingdom with the reorganized Polish army, where he had lived ever since.

Mr. MS had a thirty-year history of hospitalization and treatment for paranoid schizophrenia, the symptoms of which included auditory and somatic hallucinations and ideas of persecution. On several occasions, he had attempted violence as a consequence of his illness. On one occasion, he attacked a fellow patient while suffering from persecutory delusions. On another occasion, he was detained and treated after attempting to murder a man on the instructions of a "radar man." At the age of fifty-six, he killed a man under the delusion that the man was about to harm him with a bullet in his key, which he could transform into a pistol.

Mr. MS was then admitted to a hospital for mentally abnormal offenders, and treated with neuroleptics. However, because of his poor English, it was difficult to assess his response. Once he was interviewed in Polish, it became clear that he was still psychotic. He believed that he was still in Poland, even though his surroundings were "known to others as England." He thought that the rest of the hospital was speaking English only to trick him into thinking he was in England. This suspicion was confirmed to him when a Polish nurse spoke to him in Polish. He claimed to recognize fellow villagers and soldiers in the hospital.

Seven years after he was admitted, Mr. MS was attacked by a fellow patient. He became convinced that this patient had a pistol concealed in a black box, and that it could be fired by pressing a button. He believed the attacker was an "artificial" person who had artificial limbs and wore a mask. Despite this, he was "able to move and behave as a normal person." Because this man was "artificial," and was dangerous to others, Mr. MS thought it was his duty to kill him.

Delusions and Responsibility

What we are doing and what we believe we are doing are not always the same. It is usually by the latter that a person is morally judged — by what he believed himself to be doing, rather than what he has actually done. A person may, of course, feel guilt or shame over what he has done unknowingly; the policeman who kills an innocent teenager under the mistaken belief that he is an armed criminal reaching for a gun may feel a deep and painful regret.[2] But if he is not culpable for having made the mistake, then we do not ordinarily hold him morally responsible for what he has done. He was acting under a mistaken belief.

The importance of beliefs to the responsibility of the mentally disordered is seen most clearly in the patient with delusions. In general, delusions are irrational, usually false beliefs that are inconsistent with the cultural and educational background of the person who holds these beliefs.[3] Delusions can be found in a number of different psychiatric disorders, such as schizophrenia, bipolar affective disorder (manic-depressive disorder), and psychotic depression. Common types of delusions are delusions of grandeur, delusions of persecution, delusions of infidelity, somatic delusions ("I have knives in my body," "my heart is rotting," etc.), religious delusions, delusions of being controlled, delusions that one's thought are being broadcast or that they are being inserted into one's mind, and nihilistic delusions ("the world is going to end," "I am going to die soon," etc.). The architecture of the delusional system may also vary; the delusions of a paranoid schizophrenic, for instance, may be fragmented and chaotic, while those of a person with classical paranoia are usually internally logical and compartmentalized.[4]

We can often judge the responsibility of the deluded person in a manner similar to the way we might judge the responsibility of a person with simple false beliefs. That is, we ask whether the person was responsible for acquiring the false beliefs, and whether his action would have been justifiable if his beliefs were true. The first of these is plainly true for the person with delusions; most would bear no responsibility for acquiring their delusions, since these delusions are the product of an involuntarily suffered psychotic illness. The second, however, is more problematic. Whether a person's actions would be justifiable if his delusions were true can be a difficult matter to decide.

In some cases, when a delusion is focal and limited in scope, it may have a clear effect on the way a person perceives an action, and this fact may exonerate that person from responsibility. For example, if one person kills another under the paranoid delusion that his life is being threatened, he might, at least in some cases, be excused from responsibility. If he has acquired his delusion through no fault of his own, and if his action was justifiable under the circumstances as he believed them, then he is acting in ignorance and cannot be held responsible for his action. In such a case, the person may think that he is acting in self-defense, and killing in self-defense is generally considered morally justifiable.

For this reason most people would probably agree that Mr. MS should be excused from responsibility for the murder he committed. He seemed to be acting under the paranoid delusion that he was in imminent danger of being killed if he did not act to protect himself. Were the circumstances as he believed them to be, his action would have been justifiable.

This may be true of a number of various types of delusions. Goldstein has outlined a helpful classification of delusions relevant to criminal responsibility, based on their content.[5] For instance, delusions of external control involve the belief that one's will, feelings, and actions are being controlled by an outside force. Delusions of grandeur involve an exaggerated sense of one's own importance, often in a religious context. Delusions of persecution involve the belief that one is being harassed, attacked, or conspired against by imaginary enemies. Finally, delusions of jealousy revolve around feelings of morbid jealousy, and often involve the belief that one's sexual partner is being unfaithful. Delusions of any of these types might lead to criminal behavior, in which case it is possible that the delusions could be exculpatory.

Many cases, however, are not this clear-cut. Generally, a person's beliefs affect his actions in more subtle ways. For instance, a person may have a delusion that makes his action more understandable, but not completely justifiable. A person with the paranoid personality disorder may suspect that a person is plotting against him, but a suspicion like this would not, of course, justify taking violent action.[6] Or a person's delusions might influence her ability to foresee certain consequences of her actions. This might happen, for example, during the manic phase of a bipolar affective disorder, in which the sufferer often has feelings of extraordinary self-confidence.

Imagine, for example, that a person with the bipolar affective disorder begins to have delusions of grandeur, and comes to believe that he is a brilliant poker player. As a consequence, he gambles away all of the money that he and his wife have saved over the years, all the while believing that if he keeps playing he will multiply their savings. When we judge his responsibility for his actions, we will probably weigh in a number of different factors. We might want to know how convinced he was that he would win; we would probably be more willing to exonerate him if he thought that he had absolutely no chance at all of losing than if he merely thought that his chances of losing were fairly small. We might also ask whether his actions would have been justifiable if his delusion had been true. Gambling with his family's savings is arguably difficult to justify even if he were absolutely certain that he would win.

In other cases, a person might clearly be deluded, but it might not be so clear whether or not the delusion is a legitimate excusing condition. For example, if a person has the delusion that his thoughts and actions are being controlled by the FBI, he might believe both that his actions are wrong and that he is not accountable for them, since the choice to act was not his. Presumably, whether or not we hold him responsible for his actions will depend on the extent to which we can determine whether he has genuinely acted "freely" in this case — though under such circumstances, it will be controversial what "acting freely" involves.

A similar problem might occur with psychotic patients who are not deluded but who experience "command hallucinations": patients who hear voices telling them to behave in certain ways. If a patient hears the voice of God telling him to kill his father, should he be excused from responsibility if he follows the command? The American Psychological Association has argued that very few people who receive command hallucinations actually obey them, suggesting that command hallucinations are not usually coercive.[7] However, if the patient does follow the command, believing that terrible consequences will ensue if he does not, then this seems good reason at least to mitigate his blame.

Often a delusion will not have such a bald effect on the way a person perceives her actions, but will nonetheless color these actions in other ways. A person who believes that her thoughts are being inserted into her mind will certainly act differently than she would if she did not believe this. Knowing that this person has such a delusion will certainly help us to interpret and understand her actions. But the actual relationship between her beliefs and her actions often will not be straightforward enough for one to say precisely how these beliefs have affected the way that the person sees her actions. Similar problems arise when a person's delusions are not so focal and limited in scope. Paranoid delusions, for example, may not be limited to specific beliefs about a certain person, but may rather be a range of beliefs about persecution which cast a certain, menacing hue on the way a person sees the world. For example, the following case history would be difficult to characterize as an example of simple false belief.

Case History

Mr. GS was a 29-year-old, mildly mentally impaired man with a diagnosis of paranoid schizophrenia.[8] He was single and unemployed, and he lived with his parents. He had been treated for his schizophrenia for ten years when he attacked his mother. He believed that she became transformed into another woman (whom he disliked) every time she put on her glasses. He also believed that this woman could change into his mother, and this infuriated him still further. Mr. GS also attacked his father on one occasion, after a similar "transformation."

A poor student, Mr. GS had never been able to hold a job longer than two weeks. He was the second oldest of five children, two of whom also suffered from mental impairment and schizophrenia. His behavior had become increasingly strange around the age of seventeen. Before this time, he had been shy and solitary, but affectionate. Subsequently, he began to withdraw socially; he became hypochondriacal and preoccupied with his appearance. He was convinced that he was especially attractive. After an accidental overdose he saw a psychiatrist and claimed that he was a well-known singer. He started dressing in his sister's clothes, and once he ransacked his parents' house. He began to claim the members of his family were robots. He was admitted to the hospital four times over the next ten years, and while he responded well to neuroleptics, he did not comply well with treatment as an outpatient. In public he often thought that other people were looking at him and talking about him.

It seems plain that we cannot simply think of this man's psychotic delusions in the same way that we think of ordinary mistaken beliefs. Certainly his beliefs were mistaken — he believed that his family were robots, that they were being transformed into other people — but these mistaken beliefs do not explain or justify his actions, or at least not entirely. Mr. GS's thinking is distorted in many complex ways beyond a simple mistake of fact.

In these sorts of cases, often the best one can do is to attempt to see the patient's circumstances through her eyes and interpret her behavior accordingly. Most people are inclined to take a fairly generous attitude toward the person's responsibility in such cases, on the grounds that delusions are involuntarily acquired and may influence her actions in ways that are hard for others to appreciate. In this case, for example, the hint of rationality underlying the actions suggests that they were done out of paranoia and fear. However, these delusions and actions are so foreign to ordinary human behavior that it is clearly difficult to understand just how this man's thinking has been distorted.

Responsibility for Beliefs and Delusions

How we are likely to judge a deluded person's responsibility for her actions will be influenced by the responsibility she bears for her condition. If a person could have foreseen and avoided her condition, then plainly we will be less willing to consider her blameless for the ill effects that ensue. On the other hand, if her condition is clearly suffered involuntarily, then we will be much more willing to exonerate her from blame.

The degree of responsibility a deluded person bears for his condition varies widely. At one extreme is drug abuse. Amphetamine intoxication, for example, might cause delusions of persecution, and this is obviously a condition which the sufferer bears a considerable amount of responsibility for acquiring. At the other extreme are organic brain lesions, where the sufferer plainly carries none of the responsibility for acquiring the condition. Huntington's chorea, a genetic disorder, may have delusional thinking among its constellation of symptoms, and obviously we would not hold a person responsible for his genetic constitution.

Much more commonly, however, a delusion will arise in a condition whose etiology is unknown, as with the functional psychiatric disorders. Bipolar affective disorder and schizophrenia, for example, seem to be conditions that are largely outside the sufferer's control. Both seem to be determined to some degree by the person's genetic inheritance. Yet the sufferer often does exert some control over his condition; for example, the symptoms of both disorders can be controlled to some extent by medication.

In most cases of delusional thinking, the patient's irrational false belief is clearly a product of some sort of psychiatric condition, and because a person is generally not responsible for these conditions, she bears no responsibility for her irrational false belief. Occasionally, however, the line between delusions and other sorts of irrational false belief can grow hazy. And it is not always clear whether a person bears the responsibility for these other sorts of irrational false belief.

The clearest and most common example of an irrational false belief for which one might judge the agent responsible is self-deception. Self-deception is often characterized as "lying to oneself," or "persuading oneself to believe what one knows is not so." The mother who is so anxious for her tone-deaf son to become a successful musician that she convinces herself of his talents; the jealous husband who misinterprets his wife's behavior and persuades himself that she is having an affair; the prospective suitor who interprets the continual rejections of his beloved as a sign that she is playing hard to get: these are all examples of the sort of irrational false beliefs that are normally outside the realm of psychopathology. Indeed, self-deception is so common that without it, ordinary living would be virtually unrecognizable.

Obviously, we would be more inclined to hold a person responsible for self-deception than we would for a delusion that arose from conditions suffered completely involuntarily. But the degree to which a person should be regarded as responsible for his self-deception may also vary considerably. Some self-deceptive beliefs seem to have a near-compulsive character. For example, an insecure husband who desperately desires that his wife be faithful to him might come to believe that she is having an affair, despite her assurances and in the face of overwhelming evidence to the contrary. On the other hand, self-deception more commonly occurs in accordance with a person's desires, and it may then seem less compulsive — say, the doting mother who convinces herself of her child's virtuosity on the violin.

When we judge responsibility in ordinary circumstances, we normally assume that a person is able to examine her beliefs rationally, look at the justification for those beliefs and arrive at reasoned conclusions. A person ordinarily acquires her beliefs about important matters over a period of time, with the opportunity to scrutinize the belief, look at competing evidence, listen to arguments to the contrary, and so on. And although even ordinary, mentally sound persons frequently fail to examine their beliefs carefully, they usually have the opportunity and the ability to do so. The thought of the person with psychotic delusions is often so distorted that she is unable to put her beliefs under this sort of scrutiny. It is partly for this reason that we are generally inclined to blame a person less who has come to an irrational belief as a consequence of psychosis than the person who has come to an irrational belief in other ways.

Nonetheless, it is worth remembering that even if a person bears little responsibility for acquiring his beliefs, he still chooses whether or not to act on them. Even if a belief is compelled, it does not follow that actions based on that belief were compelled. Motivational factors also come into play. Even if an agent holds a belief A and a further belief B, the belief that all things considered, it is best that he *act* on belief A, he may still choose to refrain from acting on belief A. This might occur as a result of *akrasia*. Therefore, in judging moral responsibility, we look not solely at the factors that have resulted in a person's having come to hold a belief but also at the factors that have resulted in his choosing to *act* as he did.

Responsibility for Moral Beliefs

Occasionally, a mentally disordered person will come to hold new beliefs not about facts, as in the previous cases, but about values. As a result of illness or injury, a person will come to believe that a certain action is morally acceptable, or even obligatory (for example, the belief of Mr. MS that it was his duty to kill the "artificial" man). Sometimes these sorts of moral belief are intertwined with command hallucinations, and often they are tied to various delusions about facts. In judging responsibility, we can look at many of these sorts of moral belief in the same way that we look at factual beliefs: by examining the way in which the belief was acquired, the responsibility of the person for holding the belief, his opportunity and ability to scrutinize the belief, and so on.[9]

The sorts of moral belief that result from psychosis are often transitory, especially if they respond to medication; they are not as well-integrated with the patient's other beliefs as the moral beliefs of a mentally sound person might be; and they have not been subjected to the sort of rational scrutiny that we would expect in ordinary circumstances. However, some moral beliefs that have resulted from illness, injury, or medical intervention are more problematic, because they are stable, integrated, and susceptible to rational examination.

One procedure, for example, that often results in relatively sudden and dramatic changes in the patient's beliefs is psychosurgery. Psychosurgery is usually characterized as a surgical procedure whose aim is to correct disordered mental states by altering healthy brain tissue, often for the purpose of changing the patient's personality.[10] For example, psychosurgery will necessarily involve significant changes in the patient's personality if it is successfully to treat obsessive-compulsive disorder or uncontrollable aggression, two disorders for which psychosurgical procedures have been performed. And accordingly, it will often involve changes in the patient's moral beliefs.

A straightforward example of the sorts of changes in belief that accompany changes in personality is the "disinhibition" that often results from leucotomy, and that may also result from various frontal lobe syndromes. After leucotomy has been performed on a patient, the patient sometimes becomes less tactful and restrained, more outspoken and less self-critical. As a consequence of the surgery, one might say, the patient comes to hold different beliefs about appropriate behavior. These beliefs are relatively stable, and they accompany similar changes in the patient's personality.

Can we hold a person morally responsible when she acts on these kinds of new moral belief? It seems that we must. First, these sorts of moral belief, in contrast to the those in psychotic illness, can more properly be said to be the person's own beliefs. They are more stable, better integrated into the machinery of her character, and more easily subjected to rational examination. Of course, this may not be true of all such cases, and it is certainly possible to imagine cases where a person finds certain thoughts intrusive and alien, perhaps in the same way that a person with obsessive-compulsive disorder regards the unwelcome thoughts that are characteristic of her problem. Or, in some cases, it may seem that a person's beliefs cannot be regarded as her own because of the progressive or fluctuating nature of her disorder — as with, for instance, the progressive personality changes that might result from a growing frontal lobe tumor. In such cases, we might not regard the moral beliefs arising from this condition to be truly the person's own, for ordinarily we expect a person's moral beliefs to have a certain stability. But if the person has examined and endorsed these new moral beliefs, if she feels the identity with them that we normally expect a person to feel with her moral beliefs, then it seems that we must hold her morally responsible for acting on them.

This approach is consistent with the way that we ordinarily regard a person who is acting on his newly acquired moral beliefs. For example, if a person has changed his mind about a certain moral belief — the result, say, of a religious conversion or a loss of faith — then we do not hesitate to hold him responsible for acting on this new belief. This approach would probably also be the one taken by the agent himself. That is, a person who has acquired a new belief as a result of psychosurgery would probably regard himself as morally responsible for his actions. And if he has no relevant neurological deficits as a result of his surgery, then there seems to be little reason to disagree with him.

The second reason for regarding such persons as morally accountable is that new moral beliefs such as these cannot be said to carry the same excusing force as a factual belief. If a person acts on a mistaken belief about the facts of a situation, we generally excuse her from responsibility on grounds of ignorance. But we cannot speak as comfortably in this way about moral beliefs — about having an incorrect moral belief, or being morally mistaken. The excusing force of moral beliefs comes from their relevance to facts; if we were to attribute an excusing force to mistaken moral beliefs, it would be in relation to moral facts. But there is certainly no consensus about whether moral facts exist or what these moral facts might be, and thus no consensus on which moral beliefs are mistaken.

In some cases, however, we might well say that such a person is *justified* in acting on that moral belief — that, given his circumstances, his action was morally acceptable.[11] For while an excuse carries its force independently of the morality of the action for which the agent is excused, a justification derives its force from the moral character of the action. Normally, when a person acts in accordance with a moral belief that we do not share, we do not consider that he is acting in ignorance and that he thus should be excused. However, we do sometimes say that he is *justified* in acting as he did, given his moral beliefs. So while we may not say that the psychosurgical patient should be excused for his actions, in some cases we might well say that his actions were justified.

Ironically, it is, I suspect, an implicit acknowledgment of the stipulation that an agent's moral beliefs be "his own" for him to be held responsible that may lead one initially to think that a person should be excused for acting on these moral beliefs. In general, we are much more willing to forgive a person who breaks the law or who acts in what we regard as an immoral manner if he is acting in accordance with a sincerely held moral belief. For example, the American public seemed willing to forgive Col. Oliver North's efforts to assist the Nicaraguan *contras,* while also opposing the goals toward which he was working, ostensibly because he was acting in accordance with a sincerely held, though misguided, set of moral beliefs. In the case of a person who has come to a new moral belief as the consequence of injury or intervention, we may be inclined to excuse the person for precisely the opposite reason — because we suspect that these new beliefs are *not* the person's own. However, if the person believes that, and behaves as if, they are his own, if the beliefs are stable and well-integrated with his other beliefs, then there seems to be little ground for this suspicion.

Responsibility and Personal Identity

This discussion raises another, potentially more difficult question. If a person has, as a result of disease, trauma, or medical intervention, acquired new moral beliefs, is he accountable for his earlier actions, which were based on his old moral beliefs? Suppose, for example, that after a cerebrovascular accident a person's convictions about moral matters change dramatically. Even if we agree that he should be regarded as accountable for these new moral beliefs, should we hold him responsible for his previous actions — actions which, according to his new beliefs, he would not perform?

In an odd way, these problems turn on questions of personal identity. Philosophical convention has it that the reason we are identical (or continuous) with our past selves is that we have physical and psychological continuity with those past selves. That is, I am the same person now that I was when I was eighteen years old because I have the same body that I had then and because I am psychologically connected to that person by virtue of my memory, my personality, and various other aspects of my intellect. Which and what combinations of these physical and psychological factors are important depends on what philosophical convention one subscribes to, but nearly everyone agrees that psychological factors such as memory and personality are important. Yet, in the patient who has undergone psychosurgery, a stroke, head trauma, or whatever, psychological factors such as personality and memory may be altered dramatically. Thus, the question arises: can we regard this person as the same person that he was in the past? If not, then it seems unjust to hold him morally responsible for those past actions, which were done, as it were, by a different person.

A reasonable approach would be to hold such a person less responsible if he is dramatically different from his past self, and more responsible if he is more or less the same. It seems unfair to hold a person responsible for an action done in the past which he cannot remember and which would be completely uncharacteristic of him as he is now. This approach is consonant with our attitudes toward elderly persons who have committed crimes in their youth; one reason (among others) that we tend to be more forgiving is that we realize that they may have been very different people then. On the other hand, if the person's psychological changes are only minor ones and he is reasonably regarded as the same person, then it seems reasonable to hold him morally responsible for his past actions.

The problems of personal identity for moral responsibility in situations such as these are mainly theoretical. Psychosurgery is increasingly rare, and only very infrequently would a criminal offender undergo traumatic or illness-related psychological changes of such a degree that he should be judged a different person. However, the problems of personal identity become much more acute in cases of psychotic disorders. Often, as a consequence of a mental disorder, a person will act in ways that, even in the light of that person's psychotic beliefs, seem unjustifiable or inexcusable but that would be completely uncharacteristic of him in his nonpsychotic state. In such cases, it is not clear whether the person should be held responsible for what, during his psychosis, he has done.

Case History

Mr. S was a 25-year-old man who was arrested after trying to swindle a woman out of money from her bank account.[12] He had identified himself to her by phone as Lt. Higgins of the New York Police Department, and had explained that he was temporarily on assignment in Washington. He had tried to persuade the woman to withdraw a large sum of money from her account and give it to him, explaining that he was investigating an employee at the bank who was suspected of embezzlement. The woman became suspicious at this implausible story and called the police. When Mr. S came to her house to collect the money, he was arrested.

This was Mr. S's first and only criminal offense. He was a native of upstate New York and a graduate of an Ivy League university. He had a family history of bipolar affective disorder. Two years prior to his arrest, his brother had developed the disorder, and his maternal grandmother was also reported to have been manic-depressive. Six years earlier, his father had committed suicide, and the treating psychiatrist believed that he had probably been bipolar as well.

After graduating from college, Mr. S had worked as a carpenter, first in a suburb of New York and later in Washington, D.C. He had moved to Washington eight months prior to his arrest, after a romantic relationship with a woman had been broken off, and he may have been clinically depressed at that time. He then began to show signs of grandiose thinking. He told his mother that he was a law student (he was in fact auditing some law courses), and that he was writing a book on politics. He also described himself to her as a lobbyist for environmental causes. His former girlfriend visited him around this time and was alarmed by his grandiosity and his diminished need for sleep. She described him as a "different person."

After his arrest he had undergone a psychiatric evaluation, which recommended that he be followed by a psychiatrist. However, he was not placed on lithium for his apparent bipolar disorder. About a year later, he began to show signs of grandiosity and expansive thinking again. He began dating many women, and he developed plans to buy land, on which he wanted to build luxury homes. He missed psychiatric appointments, wrote a bad check, and violated his probation. He bought a truck with money he did not have; later, he returned the truck to the lot with an apologetic note. He was arrested in New York several months later for hitchhiking.

He was eventually placed on lithium after a depressive episode, and he responded well. His manic and depressive episodes did not reappear. He developed a relationship with a woman and continued in his job as a carpenter. He did not commit any more crimes.

Looking back on his previous offenses, Mr. S said that while he "knew" that he did not have enough money to pay for the truck, he "fooled himself" into thinking that he would have the money available before the check had cleared. He also admitted that he "knew" that his bank scam was wrong, but he had intended to repay the woman once he was financially secure.

The case of Mr. S is puzzling, because while it seems somewhat unfair to hold him morally responsible for what he did during his manic state, it is not immediately apparent why. Unlike the case of a person with focal delusions, whose actions appear somewhat reasonable — even justifiable — in the light of his delusions, the actions of Mr. S are difficult to understand. His thinking is grandiose, his actions impulsive, but we do not know why he acted as he did. In fact, his past actions seem rather opaque even to Mr. S, who admits but cannot really explain his truck theft or his botched swindle.

Mr. S was judged by the court to be legally responsible for his actions. However, his psychiatrist felt that Mr. S should have been exonerated from responsibility under the American Law Institute Model Penal Code, on the grounds that Mr. S was unable to appreciate the wrongfulness of his act. Mr. S was clearly manic-depressive; he acted wrongfully only during the manic phases of his illness; and during these manic phases, argued Ratner, his distorted judgment prevented him "from being able meaningfully to distinguish right from wrong."[13] He suggests that while Mr. S possessed a "factual" grasp of his situation, he did not have a "rational" grasp. Indeed, after the truck theft, says Ratner, "it was only as his illness remitted that it began to dawn on him that he was in trouble for breaking the law while on probation. Even then he thought by returning the slightly used truck with a note, he could cancel out the charges lodged against him."[14]

Even if it were clear just what is meant by "knowing the difference between right and wrong" (an assumption that I have questioned), the distorted thinking that Ratner describes bears no immediately apparent relationship to an ability to "appreciate wrongfulness."[15] Just what it means to have a "factual" but not a "rational" grasp of the illegality of one's actions Ratner does not explore. Certainly, Mr. S was not thinking soundly at the time of his offenses, but the sort of irrational self-deception that Ratner attributes to him — for example, convincing himself that his actions were "not really wrong" — is characteristic of many individuals who are mentally healthy. If an understanding of one's actions and their morality are the criteria for exoneration, then it seems that Mr. S must be held morally responsible for his offenses.

However, I would like to suggest that Mr. S has another avenue for exoneration open to him, based on personal identity. One reason that it seems unfair to blame him for his actions during his manic state is related to the fact that these actions seem so uncharacteristic of him. His expansive, criminal behavior came only during the manic phase of his illness. His former girl-friend even remarked that during his manic state he became a "different per-son." This seems to be the rationale for our inclination to excuse him from blame: his actions during the manic phase of his disorder do not seem to be truly his. They are, at least in some sense, the actions of a different person. And if a person's character temporarily changes very dramatically, then it seems more reasonable to treat him, from the standpoint of moral responsi-bility, as a different person.

This conclusion is not as radical as it might initially seem. If, unbeknownst to him, a person were given mind-altering drugs, and as a result began to be-have strangely, then we would not hesitate to excuse him from responsibility for his actions. Even though he may have acted intentionally at the time, his actions were not truly his. He was temporarily changed by influences over which he had no control. Likewise with Mr.S: he was changed, for a short time, by his disorder.

Three caveats need to be mentioned here, however. First, anyone can be-have uncharacteristically, and the mere presence of aberrant behavior does not mean that a person is reasonably regarded as a different person. For that, there must be clear changes in the person's character, and the relative absence of con-trol over those changes.

Second, the changes in personality and other psychological characteris-tics that result from a mental disorder will vary widely. Not all changes will be sufficient to warrant saying that a person needs to be treated morally as if she were a different person during her disorder. It is a matter for debate how much and what sort of change is sufficient.

Third, not all changes that result from a mental disorder will be sudden and temporary. With many disorders, psychological changes will appear over a period of time, and they will not be easily reversible. With others, psycho-logical disturbances appear to be so long-standing and deeply rooted in the per-son's character that they seem to be as much a part of that person as many of his other psychological characteristics. With these sorts of disturbances, it is difficult to make rigid distinctions between the "ill person" and the "well per-son," because in an important sense they are the same.

The difficulties of exonerating a person on identity-related grounds are well illustrated in the following case history of a deluded woman with schizophrenia. Although the woman is plainly very psychotic, it is not at all clear whether one would be justified in saying that she has become a "dif-ferent" person. However, it may be that she should be exonerated on other grounds.

Case History

D. J. was a white female in her early thirties arrested for the murder of a four-year-old black child.[16] A paranoid schizophrenic, D. J. said that she supported genocide and cannibalism of blacks. She believed that blacks were an inferior race to whites, who were descendants of extraterrestrial beings. D. J. thought that by killing a black person she would remind her fellow whites of their true origins and thus redress the earth's natural order.

D. J. had graduated from high school in San Francisco and married a man who was later to become a successful lawyer. In the early years of her marriage, she began to consult a psychiatrist, first for hyperventilation and later for hallucinations. Her mental condition fluctuated but gradually deteriorated over the next several years. She left her husband and took up with a businessman, had a son by him, and then left him as well. Her life gradually became more and more chaotic; she began using narcotic drugs, took up with a number of different men, and eventually had her visits with her son restricted by the courts. She was committed briefly to a mental hospital and was on anti-psychotic medication, which seemed to stabilize her thoughts; however, she did not take the anti-psychotics regularly, because she preferred her unmedicated state to her condition while she was taking the medication.

Two and a half years before the murder, D. J. was arrested for clubbing a Chinese woman on the head with a wine bottle, in an attempt to hit the child that the woman was carrying. She was hospitalized from jail, and at that time her motives for the attack were not clear. She claimed that she was under the influence of drugs at the time of the attack and did not remember the incident at all. She was given probation for assault with a deadly weapon.

The year before the murder brought several bizarre incidents. At one point, D. J. stripped naked at her mother's house, smeared herself with menstrual blood and said that she was participating in some sort of ritual. Her mother called D. J.'s psychiatrist and eventually the police, but when the police arrived, D. J. was able to convince them that hospitalization would not be necessary.

D. J. later left home and traveled to Alabama to find the Ku Klux Klan, saying that she wanted "to hear the truth directly from the source." She never reached the Klan, however, but instead spent some time looking for "the ape that went into space," a chimpanzee which had been studied by the space program and which she had heard was kept in Alabama. She eventually wound up at a mission for runaways, the director of which contacted D. J.'s mother, who in turn sent D. J. money for a bus ticket home.

About a year after her return to California, D. J. murdered the black child. She told a psychiatrist shortly afterward that she "enjoyed killing the nigger" and explained that "niggers" are not humans and were supposed to be eaten. The Chinese, she said, were spice for the stew. The psychiatrist reported that D. J. seemed emotionally elated, that her thoughts ran together and that she admitted to both auditory and visual hallucinations. She claimed that nature talked to her, but she said that no voices told her to kill the black child. She said that she strangled the boy because she saw a California state flag with a bear on it which suggested to her that she should kill with her "bare" hands.

A later examination revealed that D. J. possessed a complex delusional system of beliefs about the origins of blacks. She claimed that blacks were "put on earth, as were cows, chickens and rabbits, to be killed and eaten by people."[17] She believed that the rise of blacks in recent years to middle-class respectability defied the natural order of the world, and that she was somehow called upon to restore this order. She believed that if she had the courage to do what was clearly right, and kill a black child, others would follow her lead. Cannibalism would infuse whites with the vitality of the blacks that they ate. The examining psychiatrist noted that her illness "left her globally bizarre," and that it "undermined her critical faculties" and "impaired her judgment."[18]

After a few weeks on anti-psychotic medication, the patient's condition had improved markedly. She became less agitated, and stopped hearing nature speak to her. Even so, she still occasionally heard voices calling her name, and she held on to her racial ideas. However, she no longer believed that it was her duty to act on these beliefs. Her elation was replaced by an emotional blankness.

By her early thirties, D. J.'s schizophrenia had transformed her, at least in some sense, into a different person from the person she had been when she had married. No doubt we all change over the course of time, but these changes are ordinarily much less dramatic than D. J.'s, and are at least partly the product of our own conscious choices. It is a matter for debate whether or not the changes in D. J.'s thought and personality were sufficient for us to say that she ought to be seen morally as a different person. The resolution of that debate will depend on the extent of the changes in her personality, memory, and cognitive function — matters that are not explored fully in the case history. More important for our purposes, though, will be another problem, which relates to the prospect of reversing these psychological changes.

Even if we thought that D. J. had undergone such dramatic changes that we should regard her, morally speaking, as a different person, the question arises as to whether she has permanently *become* that different person. In contrast to the case of Mr. S, the manic-depressive man who changed radically during his manic states, D. J. has less hope of returning to any ordinary, baseline psychological state. Though she did respond to some extent to antipsychotics, she remains deluded and emotionally blank. Because her psychological changes appear more long-standing and less reversible, it is difficult to conceptualize a "true" personality underlying the schizophrenic one — or indeed, what a "true" personality might mean in such a case.

Even so, there are other plausible arguments to be made for exonerating D. J. from responsibility, despite the fact that a jury eventually found D. J. to be guilty of first-degree murder. The most plausible argument is that her delusional beliefs seem to be such that she might be excused from moral responsibility on grounds of ignorance. As grotesque as her actions might appear, they seem to be justifiable if her delusions had been true. D. J. apparently believed, first, that killing a black person was morally equivalent to killing an animal, an action that most Western societies believe is justifiable; second, that her action was part of a much larger plan, and would result in much greater good for the human race, in that it was a restoration of a natural order; and third, that in acting in this way she was acting in accordance with her moral duty. To the limited extent that her beliefs made any sense at all, they seem to justify her action.

Second, D. J.'s delusions caused her to be ignorant about the facts of what she was doing when she killed the child. What she did was radically different from what she believed herself to be doing. She mistakenly believed that she was acting in accordance with a grand plan, and that she was restoring some sort of natural order.

It is notable that, in this case, D. J.'s delusions involved both factual and moral beliefs. She had mistaken factual beliefs about her place in a grand scheme, and she had moral beliefs that, if we cannot call mistaken, are certainly somewhat unorthodox, and are different from both the moral beliefs that she held when she was on her medication and those that she had held at an earlier stage in her schizophrenia.

The factual and moral beliefs that D. J. held affected her perception of her action in different ways. Her mistaken factual beliefs affected her perception of the facts of the situation in which she acted. On the other hand, her bizarre moral beliefs affected not how she perceived the facts of her situation but how she saw her action morally. Thus, they are relevant not because they might excuse her action on grounds of ignorance but because they are what would *justify* her action if her delusions were true. Her actions seem justifiable only in the light of the fact that she believed that she was doing the moral equivalent of killing an animal, and that doing it was her moral duty. This is important for how we view her case. For even if she had had mistaken factual beliefs as a result of her delusion, we would not consider her action justifiable if she believed that she was doing a morally reprehensible thing — if, for example, she believed not that she was acting in accordance with a grand scheme to restore a natural order but that she was doing something morally evil.

Finally, however, there is another plausible argument for exonerating D. J. Some people, the severely psychotic among them, are so disordered that they lack even the minimal mental faculties necessary to be considered morally responsible agents. For this reason, we exclude them from our universe of moral relationships, whereby we attribute to a person a connection with the moral aspects of her actions. Here one might argue that D. J.'s thinking is so disordered that we cannot attribute to her even this minimal level of intellectual functioning.

However, although D. J.'s thinking is bizarrely distorted, it is not clear whether or not she is incapable of even those minimal mental abilities that we assume of morally responsible agents. She was deluded at the time of the murder, but she was capable of communicating and reasoning to some limited extent. It is a matter for discussion just what mental abilities are relevant to judgments of this sort, and this is the subject that I take up in greater detail in the next chapter.

Conclusion

A psychotic person's beliefs about her actions can affect her culpability dramatically and in a wide range of ways. In this chapter, I have tried to explore some of these ways, focusing on the deluded patient. The most common reason for exonerating a deluded patient from moral responsibility for her actions will be that, given her delusions, her actions were justifiable. However, I have also pointed out some other ways in which a psychotic patient's mental condition might affect her culpability, including issues of personal identity.

The next chapter takes up where this one leaves off, examining those patients whose mental conditions are even more severely damaged. In chapter 7, I argue that some people are so mentally impaired by their disorder that they cannot be considered morally responsible agents. These sorts of people we should view as lying outside our scheme of moral responsibility altogether.

7

The Threshold of Morally Responsible Agency

There are two widely used but conceptually different ways of approaching the moral responsibility of the psychiatrically ill person. On the one hand, psychiatric illness might be seen as an excusing condition in itself: mentally ill people are different from ordinary adults, and therefore they are not subject to our ordinary moral conventions regarding responsibility. On the other hand, one might argue that psychiatric illness excuses because it is a subclass of another type of excusing condition, such as ignorance or compulsion. According to this view, a psychiatric illness excuses only insofar as it places a person's action in one of the other categories of excusing conditions. A psychiatrically ill person might then be excused from responsibility for her actions, but only if her illness made it the case that she acted in ignorance or under compulsion.

I have suggested that neither of these views is adequate in itself. We would be mistaken to assume either that psychiatric illness is *per se* an excusing condition or that it is simply a subspecies of other excusing conditions. Psychiatric illness can function in either of these roles, as well as in some other unconventional ways.

Thus far I have concentrated mainly on the second view, the ways in which psychiatric illness can function as a subclass of other excusing conditions. I have suggested that mental illness may excuse on grounds of ignorance, as it does when a psychotic person has delusions. It may also exonerate a patient on grounds similar to compulsion, as in the case of the impulse-control disorders.

However, it is also important to realize that there are cases where a mentally ill person has acted neither in ignorance nor under compulsion but where, nonetheless, we should not hold that person morally responsible for her actions. These are cases where, as a result of mental illness, a person's mental abilities fall below the threshold that we consider necessary for a person to be a morally responsible agent. By "morally responsible agent," I mean a person who by virtue of her mental abilities we include in our scheme of moral responsibility: that realm where we ascribe a relationship between actors and the moral import of their actions. Just as we do not customarily include very young children in this realm, neither should we include those people whose mental disorders leave them without a certain minimal level of mental ability.

However, it is equally important to realize that when we regard these sorts of persons as nonresponsible, it is not because their psychiatric illness is an excuse. Rather, it is because these people do not meet even the minimal conditions by which the notion of excusing conditions applies. The notions of excuse, justification, accountability, and so on are concepts that we use to describe the moral relationships between certain sorts of persons and their actions. In general, these people are adults with a certain level of mental ability. Certain sorts of beings are excluded from this universe of moral relationships (animals and infants, for example), and are not regarded as morally responsible for their actions. The reason they are not responsible is that they lack the same sort of mental abilities that the other participants in this universe possess and which allow us to make certain assumptions about the way these participants think about their actions. For these people, the rules do not apply because they cannot play the game.

I will argue in this chapter that certain individuals are so mentally disordered that we cannot consider them participants in this moral universe. These individuals fall below the threshold of mental ability that we generally regard as necessary for a person to be considered morally responsible for his actions. I will argue further that this threshold of mental ability is not, and cannot be, sharply defined, and that we cannot point to any specific mental ability or characteristic that is sufficient to place a person above or below this threshold of moral responsibility. Rather, these capacities are more general and wide-ranging: the assumption that we make about persons whom we do consider morally responsible for their actions is simply that they think in roughly the same way that we do. With individuals who clearly do *not* think the way we do, our task is to determine whether any of the many ways in which their thinking might be impaired renders them sufficiently incapacitated that they fall below the threshold.

The best place to begin such a discussion is with case histories of two patients who arguably fall below the threshold of responsible agency. I will then turn to the main criterion put forward as the gauge for determining whether a person falls below the threshold, the criterion of rationality. Rationality, however, is not by itself a satisfactory way of describing those mental abilities or disabilities that are relevant to determining whether a person falls above or below this threshold. For this, I want to suggest, we must consider a broad range of relevant mental abilities.

Case History

Henderson and Gillespie describe a 24-year-old man admitted to the Glasgow Royal Mental Hospital in 1918, after his commanding officer in the army reported that he had been prone to uncontrollable fits of laughter and to episodes of talking to himself.[1] This man was unmarried and had been trained as a farmer. He had been healthy before enlisting, but had been wounded several times in combat before being admitted to the mental hospital. He was described as appearing "dull and stupid," prone to outbursts of laughter, and was disoriented to time and place, wrongly believing that the month was November and that he was in Edinburgh, rather than Glasgow. He said that he was mixed up, and admitted to auditory hallucinations. Two months after his admission, he attacked an attendant. At some times he seemed "dull and uninterested"; at others he became excited and hallucinatory, usually at night. On one such occasion, he claimed that he was the Kaiser. On another, he began shouting at the top of his voice, and when his physician came to the room, he leapt up, rushed toward him and demanded "the haunting voice be stilled." He often spoke incoherently. For example: "I want a —— nurse here at once, and those —— earrings, you have two sets, and your sister is wearing one. I have been on the film-screen for the last three weeks."

Later in his hospitalization he had further episodes where he would become hallucinatory and deluded. During these periods he became "completely inaccessible, violent and dangerous, and showed extreme psychomotor restlessness." Henderson and Gillespie reported that these attacks ordinarily lasted a day or two, and were "ushered in by a period of gloomy silence, with tense attitude and set facies. . . ." At the time of their report the man was quiet, emotionally blunted, seemingly content, "smiling in an inane way, solitary and difficult to occupy. . . . He does not react to painful stimuli, and has a degree of command automatism, in which he protrudes his tongue when ordered, and would allow one to put a pin through it." Often standing like a statue for long periods of time, he was able to answer simple questions promptly, if often incorrectly. Frequently he simply answered, "I don't know." The following is an example of his writing during this period:

To Be Hanged

Miss Reith, Miss Corrie, Miss Bastille, Miss Dewar, Miss Castor, Miss Provost, Miss Day, Miss Droit, Miss Jail, Mister Bleith, Mister Currie, Mister Braille, Mister Ewer, Mister Semolina, Mister Victor, Mister Diem, Mister Asylum, Mister Police [and so on through forty pairs of names.]

Case History

Robert Bradstone was a 32-year-old maintenance worker from Charleston, South Carolina, who was brought by the police to the county hospital psychiatric unit after he destroyed a display of television sets in a local electronics shop one evening after closing hours. The police reported that he had made no efforts to steal any of the sets or to escape when they arrived. He merely stood among the broken television sets mumbling incoherently to himself. He was unable to answer any questions, and the police reported that he gave nonsensical replies to their questions. The shop owner told the police that he had seen Mr. Bradstone pacing in front of the shop window in an agitated fashion earlier in the week, and that when he had approached him, he had muttered something incoherent about televisions and the CIA. When Mr. Bradstone was questioned by the psychiatric resident about what brought him to the hospital, he answered: "Four o'clock is too early. Birds are no goddamn help. Just ask Paul, if you don't believe me."

The only relative that social workers were able to locate was a sister in another state who had not been in touch with Mr. Bradstone for a number of years. She indicated that he had spent some time in a hospital psychiatric unit in the past for paranoid schizophrenia. She also said that their mother, who was no longer alive, had been in and out of psychiatric hospitals when she and her brother were children. The police believed that Mr. Bradstone had been homeless and jobless before his admission.

Criteria for Morally Responsible Agency

The minds of some patients are so disordered that they are, if not exactly a black box, at least a dark gray one: closed, private, and, for the most part, inaccessible. When the mental life of a person is so disordered that her actions and speech make no sense to us, we cannot take up the attitudes toward them that we ordinarily take toward our fellow human beings. We can no longer make the tacit assumption that they see the world in the same way that we do, that they understand their actions in the way we understand ours. They deserve our kindness and sympathy, but we cannot treat them, so to speak, as moral equals; they are incapable of participating in our world of moral relationships.

Though we can, in some limited ways, make sense of the two patients described above, their thoughts and actions are for the most part closed to us. We can catch glimpses of rationality in their violent actions and garbled speech, but we have no real understanding of what they believe and what they fear, of what they understand themselves to be doing and why. It seems plausible to say that they are incapable of the minimal degree of understanding that we normally assume of people whom we regard as morally responsible agents.

Yet, while most of us probably agree that, at least in principle, some people do not possess this minimal degree of understanding, and that these two patients are among them, not everyone would agree as to just what criteria need to be met before we can regard a person as falling below or above this threshold of responsible agency. The best place to begin such a discussion, then, would be to examine the most popular gauge for determining whether a person falls below the threshold. This gauge is that of rationality, and I will suggest that it is not in itself a satisfactory way to describe those mental abilities that are relevant to determining whether a person falls below the threshold. I will argue that for these determinations, we must consider not any single describable mental ability but rather the entire spectrum of abilities, some of which are more relevant than others.

Rationality

The most straightforward condition for moral responsibility, and one that is often put forward in the criminal law, is rationality. The rationality criterion appears disarmingly simple: a person cannot be held morally responsible for his actions if he is incapable of rational thought and conduct. Unfortunately, however, the notion of rationality is complex and vague enough to make its practical interpretation rather puzzling, and as a consequence, it is particularly difficult to use as a criterion for moral responsibility.

Ordinary use of the word *rational* is not precise; we might variously describe as rational a person's thoughts, emotions, actions, beliefs, desires, or even the person himself, and in each case we may mean something different. All of the varying ways in which "rational" is used contribute to the various strands of meaning which the word might reasonably be said to contain.

One strand in this use is the rational as *reasonable*. We use the term in this way more often when we speak of the rationality of persons, rather than actions. This is what we are getting at, for instance, when we say that a person has a good head on his shoulders. We may mean that he is sensible, a sound thinker; or that he makes decisions carefully and not impulsively; or even merely that his mind is functioning normally. This is the hypothetical "reasonable man" often used in law. To say, then, that a person is rational in this sense is to say that we consider him to resemble, to some extent, what we consider to be a reasonable person.

On the other hand, a separate strand in the notion of the rational applies less to persons than to actions. This is the rational as the *self-interested*. Thus, we label an action irrational if it seems likely to lead to the agent's harm, or rational if it will bring about some benefit. This sense of rationality, maximization of self-interest, seems also to be the sense in which rationality is often used in economic theory.

Finally, we have the rational as the *comprehensible*. This sense of rational we perhaps apply more easily to actions than to persons, though it may refer to either. We might say, for example, that an action is rational when we find it understandable — or, perhaps more frequently, irrational when we do not. We might call an act of vandalism irrational, for instance, but an act of embezzlement rational, meaning that we can identify with or understand the latter in a way that we cannot with the former. Here the irrational becomes the senseless, the incomprehensible, the unintelligible: that which we despair of understanding.

It should be evident why this ordinary sense of rationality is an inadequate condition for moral responsibility; a person might be rational in one sense of the word and not in another. That is, a person's actions might be comprehensible but not self-interested, as when a person acts altruistically. Or a person might be, in general, a reasonable person, but on one occasion act incomprehensibly.

The imprecision with which "rational" is used in ordinary language may contribute to the confusion with which the term is employed in a more technical, philosophical sense. The "capacity for rational thought and behavior" covers quite a lot of ground, and it is often unclear to what extent and in what ways a person's thoughts and behavior might be considered irrational. Probably the best place to begin a discussion of rationality in this more technical sense is where it is most widely used by mental health workers, and where there is the most widespread agreement as to its use — that is, in regard to the rationality of beliefs.

Delusions and Irrational Beliefs

In clinical situations, the question of whether a belief is irrational arises most often in relation to delusions. Delusions are fixed, usually false, beliefs which are not amenable to change with respect to evidence, and which are usually interpreted as a sign of psychosis. Delusions are generally not hard to identify;

what is harder is explaining just what makes a belief delusional, and how this relates to rationality.

While delusions are usually false, fixed, irrational, and indicative of psychosis, no one of these conditions is in itself sufficient (and some not even necessary) to qualify a belief as a delusion. First, although the term "delusion" is rarely used except in relation to psychosis, the presence of psychosis cannot, of course, be the sole reason why we say that a given belief is delusional. For example, a psychotic person possesses other beliefs that are not delusional; something about a particular belief, apart from the mental condition of the person who holds it, makes us recognize it as delusional. Also, we use the presence of delusions as a diagnostic marker for psychosis. We could not identify psychosis by the presence of delusions if the sole reason for saying that a belief is a delusion were the fact that the person who holds it is psychotic.

Second, although a delusion is usually false, it need not necessarily be false. Some people with paranoid delusions genuinely are being persecuted, and some men with jealous delusions really do have wives who are cheating on them.

Third, while delusions are generally fixed, so are many nondelusional beliefs. Religious beliefs, for example, seem to be fixed beliefs that are not amenable to change with regard to evidence. Being "fixed" might therefore be necessary for a belief to qualify as a delusion, but it is by no means sufficient.

The most problematic criterion for delusion, however, is the condition that the belief be irrational. There are two difficulties with this condition: first, though we can easily identify certain beliefs as irrational, we often have difficulty formulating the conditions that make those beliefs irrational; and second, though irrationality is a necessary condition for a belief to be considered a delusion, it is plainly not a sufficient condition. For example, one common sort of irrational belief that is not a delusion is self-deception — a husband so desperately in love with his wife that he continues to believe that she is faithful to him despite overwhelming evidence to the contrary, or a cigarette smoker who continues to believe that smoking will not damage his health.

Most explanations of what makes a belief rational or irrational point to some sort of contradiction between the belief and the evidence for that belief. One such explanation is given by Culver and Gert, who stipulate that, for a belief to be considered to be irrational, that belief must be contrary to the overwhelming evidence available to the person holding the belief.[2] They also suggest that an irrational belief is person-dependent; a belief that is irrational for one person may not be irrational for another. "A belief is irrational only if it is held by a person with sufficient information to know that it is false."[3] So what is an irrational belief for one person may be merely a mistaken belief for another; a belief in Santa Claus is rational for a four-year-old but irrational for an adult.

However, this formulation cannot account very well for religious and mystical beliefs. Under these conditions such beliefs might well be considered irrational, even though they are held by a great number of people. This is because religious and mystical beliefs are usually held for reasons other than grounds of evidence, so conditions for irrationality which depend on examining evidence would seem necessarily to count these sorts of beliefs as irrational.

To side-step this problem, Culver and Gert stipulate that to qualify as irrational, the fact that a belief is contradicted by the overwhelming available evidence must be obvious to almost everyone else with similar knowledge and intelligence. Thus, one cannot say that a religious belief is irrational if it is held by a large number of people.

There is an obvious problem with this stipulation, of course. If one person's belief can be deemed irrational on the grounds that it is a belief in the face of evidence to the contrary, then why should not a belief held by *many* persons in the face of evidence to the contrary? By this criterion, any belief, no matter how bizarre or contrary to evidence, is rational as long as enough people hold the same belief.

Culver and Gert's explanation avoids the real problem with using the weight of evidence as the condition for rationality of a belief. Some beliefs, religious and mystical beliefs among them, seem to have little to do with evidence. For that reason, if we want to say that these beliefs are rational — or even merely that they are not completely irrational — we will need some sort of criterion for rationality other than one that rests on the weight of evidence.

One might, of course, abandon any attempt to base the rationality of beliefs on the weight of evidence and base it entirely on the consistency of these beliefs with the beliefs held by others in the same society. However, this approach is just as problematic; some beliefs seem to be clearly rational, even though the rest of society does not share them. Rationality should entail more than mere conformity.

Furthermore, the rationality of some beliefs often has less to do with factors such as the weight of evidence and its consistency with other persons' beliefs than it does with the relationship of that belief with the person's other beliefs.[4] We usually expect a person's beliefs to have some order and consistency. Thus, we sometimes call a belief irrational not because it flies in the face of evidence but because it contradicts another of the person's beliefs. Of course, this does not mean that the inconsistency or incoherence of a belief with the person's other beliefs is enough to qualify that belief as irrational. That is, a person may hold a belief that seems clearly irrational, but that is still consistent with that person's other beliefs. For instance, the complex belief systems that schizophrenic people often possess are sometimes internally consistent, but few of us would argue that these beliefs are rational.

However, despite all these problems in defining delusions, psychiatrists generally have very little trouble *identifying* delusions. They may not be able to define a delusion, but they know one when they see it. And, to a lesser extent, the same goes for quite a number of other irrational beliefs. Most of us can agree that certain sorts of belief are rational and others irrational, even if we disagree about some outlying and borderline cases.

What should be plain here is that even in one of the clearest and most well-examined areas of psychiatry, that of delusions and belief, rationality is still a very murky concept. Saying just why a belief is irrational is a very difficult affair. And even in cases where we can agree that a belief is irrational, the question remains whether the person who holds that irrational belief is capable of rational thought and conduct. A person with an irrational belief, even a full-blown delusion, may be capable of conducting her life without difficulty except in the area that concerns her delusion. She might even have an elaborate delusional system of beliefs that have little effect on her daily living. Even when a person has a number of irrational beliefs, she may be far above the threshold of mental ability which we consider necessary for morally responsible agency.

The Rationality of Desires

It seems slightly odd to call a desire irrational. Normally we do not think that to desire something could be called irrational, or even rational; we simply desire some things and do not desire others. Desires are things that the adjectives "rational" and "irrational" seem ill-suited to describe. Even so, some desires seem to test the limits of that generalization. The compulsive desire to wash one's hands, even to the point where the skin is peeling off, may not be, strictly speaking, "irrational," but it seems to come pretty close.

Hume was suspicious of the idea that desires could be called rational or irrational. He argued that nothing could be contrary to truth or reason unless it had a *reference* to it, and because only judgments of understanding (or beliefs) have this reference, only they can be judged rational or irrational. For Hume, only in two ways could a desire be called irrational (or unreasonable, as he puts it): first, if it is based on the supposition of something that does not exist; or second, if, on the occasion when we are putting a desire into action, we choose inappropriate means for the ends we desire and deceive ourselves when we judge causes and effects. Hume says: "In short, a passion must be accompanied by some false judgment, in order to its being unreasonable; and even then tis not the passion, properly speaking, which is unreasonable, but the judgment."[5]

Under Hume's formulation, then, I might be said to have an irrational desire only if it is based in some way on a false (or better, an irrational) *belief*.

And even then, it is really the belief that is irrational, not the desire. Desiring is *itself* neither rational or irrational. Hence Hume's famous comment:

> Tis not contrary to reason to prefer the destruction of the whole world to the scratching of my finger. Tis not contrary to reason for me to choose my total ruin, to prevent the least uneasiness of an Indian or a person completely unknown to me.[6]

It does seem to most of us, though, that some sorts of desire are significantly *different* from others, even if is not clear whether they ought to be called irrational. For example, we might say this about desires that a person permits to interfere excessively with the satisfaction of other desires — say, a money-hungry executive who permits his lust for wealth to destroy his family life, which he readily admits to be more important. Or, in psychopathology, we might also suspect of being irrational those desires about which (as Feinberg argues) one has little insight. We might also want to term irrational those desires that are excessively strong, or that are self-destructive. The exhibitionist, the zoophiliac, the kleptomaniac, the compulsive hand washer, the anorexic: all these patients have desires that are out of the ordinary, and which some might call irrational on one or another of these grounds.

However, while we can certainly see that there is something unusual about these sorts of desires, it is still not uncontroversial to say that any of the standards I have enumerated above qualifies a desire as *irrational*. To say, for example, that a desire interferes with the satisfaction of other desires is not really to say anything significant about the desire itself. Many of our desires conflict with each other, and satisfying one will often frustrate the other. If a person *acts* on a desire while knowing that this will interfere with the satisfaction of more important desires, we might want to say that this is irrational, but this is calling the *action* irrational, not the desire.

Moore argues that one criterion for rationality of desires is logical consistency with other desires.[7] But this criterion is very weak; it requires only that desires not *necessarily* contradict each other. For example, the consistency condition would make a person's desire to help others irrational only if that person also had a simultaneous desire *not* to help others. Moore's formulation also oversimplifies the structure of our desires. In a sense, we have desires both for and against something very frequently; I might well want a plate of barbecue for one reason (the taste) but not want it for another (my health). We could call this irrational, but that would do little to distinguish run-of-the-mill "irrational desires" from those that seem (to most of us) truly strange, such as necrophilia or compulsive counting.

Similar difficulties emerge when we appeal to a person's lack of insight into the origin of his desire. Freud has taught us too much about our capacity for keeping the sources of our desires hidden to permit us to require complete self-awareness as a criterion for rationality. Likewise, nothing about a desire's strength *per se* makes it irrational. If we are to say that a desire is too strong, or too weak, then we must say something *else* about it: *what about it* makes it irrational for it to be too strong or too weak? If we cannot say that it is irrational for a desire to be present or absent, then *a fortiori* we cannot say that it is irrational for it to be strong or weak.

The nub of the problem with calling a desire irrational seems be related to our inability to say that a desire is incorrect.[8] Those *beliefs* that we are most likely to call irrational usually *are* incorrect; they seem irrational because they are incorrect, and so obviously incorrect that anyone should be able to see that they are incorrect. "Incorrect," however, seems an inappropriate way to describe a desire, even a desire such as a handwashing compulsion.

Although some desires are dependent on other, more basic desires, at their most fundamental level, desires do not really seem to be subject to question. We often cannot change them; we do not really have reasons for having them; and usually, we do not question them. This may have been part of what Aristotle meant when he remarked that we deliberate only about "means" and not about "ends": some fundamental desires, the "ends" of our actions, resist rational scrutiny. There seems to be no good answer, for example, to the question why we want to be happy, or why we do not like pain.

Rationality and Emotion

A further problem with using rationality as a criterion for moral responsibility is the role in our thinking and behavior of the emotions. Psychiatric disorders often affect a person's emotions much more than they affect her powers of reason. For example, schizophrenia often causes a severe flatness of affect, or a blunting of the schizophrenic person's emotions. If we use rationality as the condition for moral responsibility, then it appears we must either exclude emotional disorders or show how they can be considered within the scope of rationality.

The first alternative we can rule out. Emotions play such a large part in moral decisions that it would be unreasonable to dismiss disorders of the emotions as irrelevant to responsibility. A decision is always made within a network of values and emotions as well as beliefs, desires, intentions, and so on. To suggest that only one's powers of reason are necessary for moral decision making would be naive, if powers of reason are meant to include only the manipulation of information, memory, and so on. A person's mood will radically change how she values certain results of her possible actions. For example, a new mother suffering from post-partum depression may come to believe that she is unable to take care of the child or unable to love it; she may even become psychotic, believing that the child is dead or defective.[9] Emotional problems are such an integral part of many psychiatric disorders that in a practical sense it would be nearly impossible to discount their effects on decision-making.

Yet equally problematic is the second alternative: showing how the emotions can be included under the umbrella of rationality. Rationality is a term most often used in opposition to, rather than as descriptive of, the emotions. If we are to argue that emotional disorders are relevant to assessments of responsibility on the grounds that some emotions are irrational, then these emotions will be irrational in a sense of the term very different from that used in most other contexts.

This is not to say that the emotions have no order. It is only because we recognize some emotions as inappropriate that we are able to say that the schizophrenic or the manic-depressive person's emotions are disordered. Most people are consistent in the sorts of emotion that they feel in given situations, and it would be odd for a person to feel guilty about an action on one occasion and proud of an identical act on another occasion. It has even been argued that there are *correct* emotions to feel in a given situation; Aristotle, for example, observed that in some situations we are inclined to say that a person ought to get angry.

But it stretches the notion of rationality to describe these characteristics of emotions as rational. We can describe emotions as consistent with each other, or consistent over time, or as consonant with the emotions of other persons, but to say that an emotion is irrational seems to require that we have some notion of the ends of human behavior, some ultimate goal in the light of which an emotion (or even a desire) might be said to be rational or irrational. We find it difficult to say why an emotion can be rational when we lack such an end, or when we are unsure what that end might be.

The Rationality of Action

By far, the most extensively discussed and commonly cited criterion for responsibility is rationality of action. Though the question of what constitutes rational or irrational action is too broad-ranging and complex to deal adequately with here, it should be helpful to look briefly at some of the problems in answering that question, focusing especially on the problems the question poses for a formulation of moral responsibility.

A common manner of discussing rational and irrational action focuses on a belief-desire syllogism. In its most simple form: if I desire X and believe that action A will lead to X, then to A is rational, and not to A is irrational (assuming, of course, no other competing desires or beliefs that might interfere, and so on.)

The problem of weakness of will is a standard example of irrationality in this sense. If I want to live a long and healthy life, and I believe that to lead a long and healthy life I must stop smoking, and if I in fact decide that, all things considered, it is *best* that I stop smoking, then to continue to smoke will be an irrational action.

Discussing rationality in these sorts of terms presents a few ground-level problems for a scheme of responsibility. First, these formulations simplify an extraordinarily complex problem; it is in practice nearly impossible actually to prune away all of the many factors (conscious and unconscious) that affect actions and decisions and to analyze an action in such pure terms. Second, this formulation focuses only on a single action; sometimes an action seems irrational only in relation to a person's other actions.

The third and most important problem with this formulation, however, is a difficulty common to most formulations of rational action. In the sense of "rational" implied by this formulation, it seems appropriate only to describe an action as rational or irrational in relation to some given end. If I have a given end, such as a desire, then I can describe my action as rational or irrational if I believe that it will or will not lead to that end. However, I cannot say that the ends themselves are rational or irrational.

This leads to a couple of problems. Some actions seem irrational because of the ends they will lead to, not because they are contrary to the end that the agent desires. Wearing one's trousers on one's head for no other reason than for the sake of the action itself seems irrational in some sense of the word, but it does not seem irrational because it is contrary to some desired end; it seems irrational because wearing one's trousers on one's head seems like an irrational end to pursue.

On the other hand, it is equally if not more difficult to say what ends are rational and why, because it seems to entail postulating an end that is rational for all humans to pursue (or, conversely, some end that is irrational for all humans to pursue). However, no candidate for a rational "end" for human living seems to encompass all of the ends for which human beings do in reality act; and there seems to be no way to argue convincingly that some of these ends for which humans do actually act are rationally justified or unjustified. For example, a popular candidate for the rational "end" of human living is self-interest. However, in reality people do sometimes act contrary to their self-interest, and it is difficult to show exactly *why* we should regard these actions as irrational.[10]

Another approach to determining whether an action is rational focuses on an action's intelligibility; an action is rational if it is intelligible or understandable. Yet there are difficulties with this approach as well. It makes the rationality of an action dependent not on anything intrinsic to the action but on the interpretations of others. Thus, it will make some actions irrational because of the limits of other persons to understand ends that they do not share.

There is also the difficulty of determining what constitutes intelligibility. If it merely means understandable, then I find the actions of the cardiologist who smokes cigarettes intelligible, but I would hesitate to call them rational. On the other hand, sometimes intelligible means only consistent. And in this sense, the actions of a machine or an animal might be called rational. Also, of course, a person might consistently act irrationally.

Sufficiently Like We Are

Though they are in many ways quite different, the various senses of "rationality" as a criterion for the threshold of morally responsible agency point toward the same question. That is, is this person like us? The reason we want to know whether a person is capable of acting rationally, or of forming rational beliefs, or of acting intentionally, or of doing anything else, is that we want to know if this person is like we are to an extent sufficient for us to include them in our universe of morally responsible agents. This universe is composed of persons who share, in the broadest possible sense, certain more or less similar beliefs, assumptions, practices, activities, relationships, and so on. In this universe we have a roughly just and consistent way of connecting persons — ordinarily (but not exclusively) mentally sound adults — with the moral aspects of their actions. What we want to know about psychiatrically disordered persons is whether they are sufficiently like these persons — like ourselves — to be justly included in this universe.

When we attempt to decide whether we should include psychiatrically disordered persons in this universe, we need to know whether they have the mental capacities necessary for responsible agency. To answer this question, we need to ask what capacities *we* have that are necessary for responsible agency. And, in general, we point toward capacities such as the ability to think rationally, the ability to deliberate and form intentions and so on, because they seem to capture something of the way we think and the way we act in ways relevant to responsibility.

However, it is important to realize that *none* of these capacities can capture all (or even most) of what goes into the vast and complex process of thinking and acting. Often we act rationally, but frequently we act irrationally. We sometimes act for clear motives, but often our motives are hidden deeply in the unconscious. We sometimes ponder deeply over a problem, but often we act impulsively. Sometimes reason governs our actions, but at other times the passions prevail. It would be futile to attempt to devise a theory of human thought and behavior that captured all of the subtleties and complexities relevant to moral responsibility. Even if it were possible, a person's thinking can be impaired in so many immensely different but morally relevant ways that they would be impossible to number.

The threshold for morally responsible agency must be an assessment of global mental capacity. Aspects of this capacity include abilities such as those mentioned earlier, but no specific ability will be able to encompass all of the mental abilities necessary for morally responsible agency. Clearly, some mental abilities are more important than others, and the specific impairments of the psychiatrically disordered should be considered and weighted accordingly. However, attempting to outline necessary and sufficient conditions for the mental abilities necessary for morally responsible agency will be like attempting to devise necessary and sufficient conditions for being a person. There will always be cases on the borderline which call the conditions into question, and with which the conditions must deal, and which are, in fact, the reason for devising the conditions in the first place.

Thomas Reid and Common Sense

The question of what mental faculties are necessary for morally responsible agency is not a new one. Thomas Reid addressed the question and gave a surprisingly simple answer. Reid said that the intellectual faculty necessary for accountability was common sense, and that whether a person has common sense is easily discernible by a judge or jury. Of common sense, Reid wrote, "It is this degree of reason, and this only, that makes a man capable of managing his own affairs, and answerable for his conduct towards others."[11] Reid then goes on to say:

> The laws of all civilized nations distinguish those who have this gift of heaven and those who have it not. The last may have rights which ought not to be violated, but, having no understanding in themselves to direct their actions, the laws appoint them to be guided by the understanding of others. It is easily discerned by its effects in men's actions, in their speeches, and even in their looks; and when it is made a question, whether a man has this natural gift or not, a judge or jury, upon a short conversation with him, can, for the most part, determine the question with great assurance.[12]

What does Reid mean by common sense? The faculty of common sense, argues Reid, is an aspect of our powers of reason. However, common sense should be distinguished from reason, in that "[t]he first is to judge of things self-evident; the second to draw conclusions that are not self-evident from those that are."[13]

Common sense, says Reid, is the ability to see the self-evident. Reid thought that it was self-evident that everything of which I am conscious exists, that the thoughts of which I am conscious are mine, that those things happened which I remember, and so on. One reason why only this basic level of reason, common sense, is necessary for accountability seems to be that, according to Reid, "in the greatest part of mankind no other degree of reason is to be found."[14]

Though there are problems with Reid's simple approach, several of his points are worthy of careful note. First of all, Reid clearly means to count as below the threshold of moral agency only those persons with very limited intellectual faculties. He indicates that he is speaking of those persons who "must be guided by the understanding of others." Below the threshold would be only those persons unable to "judge the self-evident," and this would include very few people indeed. Few people would qualify as unable to realize the sorts of self-evident idea that Reid offers as examples: that their thoughts are theirs, that those things happened which they remember, and so on. The persons so mentally impaired that they unquestionably fall below this sort of threshold would be persons like the severely psychotic (chronic schizophrenics, for example), the severely autistic, and the severely demented and mentally retarded. Those with less severe disorders, such as a person with less severe psychosis, might or might not fall below the threshold. However, there is no question that the great majority of persons with psychiatric problems would indisputably be above the threshold: all of the personality disorders (including the antisocial personality, or psychopath), the anxiety disorders, most types of depression, the impulse-control disorders, the psychosexual disorders, and many others.

This part of Reid's formulation seems reasonable. If we are truly attempting to judge which people are so mentally disordered, so unlike a sound-thinking adult that they should be entirely excluded from our system of moral responsibility, then we will exclude only those with very severe disorders. The psychiatrically disordered will generally fall on some sort of continuum between those persons who clearly ought to be included in our universe of responsible agents and those whom we all agree do not. Ordinary adults clearly belong in, animals and infants clearly do not, and children, according to age, intelligence and maturity, fall somewhere along the continuum. The psychiatrically disordered and mentally impaired will be closer to one end or the other, and in a sense our task is to say whether, mentally, they are more like ordinary adults or more like infants and animals. Only the severely disordered will fall into the latter category. For example, this 23-year-old man with schizophrenia described by Henderson and Gillespie would very likely fall below the threshold of responsible agency:

> He expressed the belief that the doctors and nurses could manipulate their shadows, and that there was another person in his bed. Later he complained of tasting soap in his mouth and of receiving poison from the post beside his bed. At times he . . . chewed the end of his tie and hoarded rubbish. For weeks on end he would be in a stupor. . . . On occasion he clowned in a crude way and would walk on his hands.[15]

A second important point from Reid's account is the fact that Reid does not attempt to show why common sense is necessary for responsible agency. He does not claim that any of the self-evident truths that he lists are *themselves* in any way necessary for responsibility. Rather, he takes a lack of common sense to be an *indicator* that a person should not be considered a responsible agent.

This approach is often the way that we intuitively make these sorts of judgment — not by trying to determine whether a person possesses a specific mental ability that we have judged necessary for responsible agency, but by trying to judge the general state of the person's mental functioning. Indeed, the specific self-evident truths that Reid cites seem arbitrary, and they would doubtless strike most contemporary psychiatrists as somewhat bizarre. However, the purpose of the criteria Reid cites is roughly the same as the purpose of a psychiatrist's mental status exam under similar circumstances: to obtain a general idea of the person's mental functioning. And the results of the mental status exam are important not so much because there is anything specific that is being tested for but because the results give a more general indication of whether a person can be considered a responsible agent.

The final point worth noting from Reid's account is his suggestion that deciding who cannot be held accountable for their actions can be done by judges and juries with ease. Though the heated controversy in recent years about the insanity plea would seem to belie this argument, it should not be dismissed out of hand. One psychologist recently commented: "Madness is like obscenity: to paraphrase a former Supreme Court Justice, one need not be an expert to recognize it."[16] Often we can recognize that a person is so mentally disordered that he cannot be regarded as a morally responsible agent, but we cannot express with any precision why we recognize this. Few would argue, for example, that the patient with advanced Alzheimer's disease who wanders into the street unclothed should be regarded as a morally responsible agent, but we may still find it difficult to express exactly why he should not be considered a responsible agent. Is it because he is acting irrationally? Because he did not know that what he was doing might be offensive to others? Because he did not intend to act as he did? All of these seem to capture something of the reason why we would say that he is not a responsible agent, but each reason seems to be secondary to the judgment itself. We simply recognize that this person is impaired in enough ways to render him insufficiently like other persons to be included with them in a scheme of moral responsibility.

Judging what sorts of person fall above and below the threshold of responsible agency is best made by an educated and informed clinical examination. Nonetheless, it is often helpful to have formal criteria for judgments of this sort, not as necessary or sufficient conditions for responsible agency but as reminders of the sorts of mental ability that ought to be taken into account. A similar type of activity is that of judgments of competence to make medical decisions. These judgments are made routinely by clinicians who must decide whether patients are mentally capable of making decisions about their medical care. Physicians generally do not make these judgments of competence by reference to formal rules, but neither are the judgments arbitrary, and writers in medical ethics have proposed criteria to guide these judgments. The sorts of ability necessary for making medical decisions are general ones, and ones that common sense would suggest are relevant.

A widely used set of criteria for patient competence that would serve equally well for judgments of the threshold of morally responsible agency is that proposed by a U.S. President's Commission Report. The guidelines suggested by the commission are that the patient (1) possess a set of values and goals, (2) be able to communicate and understand information, and (3) be able to reason and deliberate about her choices.[17]

These guidelines are reasonable. Although decisions about various sorts of action will require correspondingly different mental abilities, most decisions of moral importance will require the general abilities that the commission sets out. In general, a person needs some sort of structure of goals and values to evaluate actions as good or bad, better or worse. The ability to understand, communicate, and manipulate information is necessary for most social interaction. And the ability to reason and deliberate is necessary for most actions that are taken thoughtfully rather than impulsively.

The mental capacities that one might look for in deciding morally responsible agency will be similarly forthright. One will be interested in the sorts of ability that I have discussed — rational beliefs and actions, moral values, emotions roughly like those that most persons possess. One will also be interested in abilities similar to those relevant to competence: the ability to communicate, to deliberate, to manipulate information, to have some degree of knowledge about one's actions. Clearly these abilities may change over time, and judgments of moral responsibility will be primarily concerned with the agent's abilities at the time that he acted and during the time leading up to his action.

Determining whether a given individual is enough like an ordinary adult in enough relevant ways to be counted above the threshold for morally responsible agency will not be as simple as Reid suggests. However, it is a judgment of which an educated adult is certainly capable, and which we in fact make routinely in our moral dealings with children and demented elderly persons. In these situations, we ask ourselves whether the person in question is sufficiently like an ordinary adult — sufficiently like we are — to be considered a part of our moral community. In some cases the answer will be yes, and in those cases we will use the language of praise, blame, intentionality, and so on. But in other cases the answer will be no. This does not mean that we have no moral duties toward such persons, of course. In the same way that we have duties toward others who live outside the community of morally responsible agents, such as young children, we also have duties toward those who live outside that community by virtue of their mental disorders. Whatever our duties to them, however, we cannot ascribe to them responsibility for their actions. This is not because they are excused from responsibility, but because we cannot describe their actions using the same language of excuse and accountability that ordinarily accompanies judgments of moral responsibility.

Final Remarks

Now that we have reached the conclusion of the book, it might be useful to take stock of where we have come from and how we got here. As I suggested at the beginning, part of the aim of the book has been to take what is to many people a very hazy and confused subject, the accountability of mentally ill offenders, and impose on that subject some sense of order. This I called a type of moral taxonomy. The taxonomy that I have argued for is based loosely (but only loosely) on the version of Aristotle's account of responsibility that Mackie calls the "straight rule of responsibility": that a person is morally responsible for all and only her intentional actions.

The picture that I hope has emerged from this account is one where judgments of moral responsibility are judgments about a *connection* between an agent and his action. If this connection is present, then a person deserves the moral credit for the action — the praise or the blame, for instance. But if the connection is absent, then the moral credit for the action does not belong to the agent. Following on Aristotle's account of voluntariness, there are two types of condition where a person may have "acted" but where that connection between agent and action is absent: conditions where the agent has acted in ignorance, or where he has acted under compulsion.

Now, the general stance I have tried to argue for is one in which judgments about the responsibility of mentally ill offenders are based roughly on this broad scheme of responsibility. Accordingly, there are three general ways in which person's mental illness can excuse her from responsibility: if she has acted in ignorance, if she has acted under compulsion, or, as I have argued in this last chapter, if her illness is so severe that we can no longer consider her a morally responsible agent. This is an oversimplification, of course, as the preceding chapters will have made abundantly clear. How things play out for actual mental disorders is much more complicated.

But I have tried to point out just where things get complicated, and to suggest some ways of thinking about those complications. Take, for example, Aristotle's two broad excusing conditions of ignorance and compulsion. There are mental illnesses which affect people in ways that correspond to these two excusing conditions. Persons with psychotic illnesses such as schizophrenia may have false beliefs as a consequence of their delusions, and for that reason may act in "ignorance" of what they are doing. Persons with other mental disorders, such as impulse-control or psychosexual disorders, may feel "compelled" to act in certain ways. I have argued that some persons with these disorders may legitimately be excused from responsibility for their actions. However, while it is useful to think about these kinds of disorders as species of ignorance or compulsion, this is only a start; the actual disorders are much more complicated, as I have tried to point out.

One type of disorder that I have argued should *not* be an excuse, in general, are the personality disorders. This is because, unlike many of the other disorders I have considered, a personality disorder does not break the connection between agent and action: the person with a personality disorder ordinarily *intended* to act as he did. For these actions he deserves the moral credit. I did suggest one possible exception to this rule, however, and that exception is the psychopath. The psychopath is exceptional because he does not appear to understand fully the moral aspects of his actions. Without understanding the moral aspects of one's actions, one cannot be held fully responsible for them.

Finally, the book's last chapter deals with persons who are so mentally disordered that they fall outside our scheme of responsibility altogether. If, as I have argued, responsibility hinges on intention, then a necessary precondition for responsibility will be the ability to act intentionally. Some mental illnesses, such as severe, chronic schizophrenia, affect a person's thinking in such a way that we would have difficulty saying she has acted intentionally. Persons with these disorders cannot be held responsible for their actions, because the concept of responsibility assumes capabilities that they do not possess.

Notes

Introduction

1. This is a simplification, but some of the complexities will emerge in chapter 1.
2. Insanity Defense Work Group (1983), p. 685.

Chapter 1

1. *Report of the Committee on Mentally Abnormal Offenders* (1975), p. 217.
2. Ibid.
3. Goldstein and Marcus (1977), p. 154.
4. Ibid., p. 156.
5. Finkel (1988), p. 30.
6. Zilboorg (1943), p. 273.
7. *Report of the Committee on Mentally Abnormal Offenders* (1975), p. 218.
8. Finkel (1988), p. 28.
9. Ibid., p. 31.
10. Moore (1984), p. 219.
11. Insanity Defense Work Group (1983), p. 685.
12. Goldstein and Marcus (1977), p. 165.
13. Finkel (1988), p. 35.
14. Abrams (1980), p. 446.
15. Goldstein and Marcus (1977), p. 165.
16. Finkel (1988), p. 34.
17. Ibid.
18. Ibid.
19. Ibid.
20. Goldstein and Marcus (1977), p. 165.

21. Abrams (1980), p. 446.
22. Moore (1984), p. 231.
23. Ibid.
24. Abrams (1980), p. 447.
25. Ibid.
26. Such a lesion could of course be *diagnosed* by means other than observing the patient's behavior, but it is not clear whether these diagnostic tests would be counted as a "manifestation" of the disease. If they are in fact counted as a manifestation, then the A.L.I. test would have the problem of dealing with some of the potential tests for diagnosing psychopaths, such as EEGs.
27. Finkel (1988), p. 12.
28. *Report of the Committee on Mentally Abnormal Offenders* (1975), p. 241.
29. Ibid., p. 244.
30. Moore (1982), p. 226; Dennett (1973), pp. 157–85.
31. Silva et al. (1989), p. 7.
32. One might even argue that the violent person with a tumor should be regarded as falling into this class of beings. To hold the violent person with a tumor responsible for his actions might be considered unjust, because his brain functions in such a different way from ours that we cannot make the same sorts of assumptions about his intentions, his will, his desires, and so on that we can make about persons without tumors. He is different from us in such a way that to regard him as one of us in our system of responsibility would be unfair.

Chapter 2

1. *Nicomachean Ethics* iii.1.30–5.
2. *Nicomachean Ethics* iii.1.1111a21–4.
3. *Nicomachean Ethics* iii.1.1110b1.
4. *Nicomachean Ethics* iii.1.1110a11–13.
5. *Nicomachean Ethics* iii.1.1110a17–19.
6. *Nicomachean Ethics* iii.1.1110a28–31.
7. *Nicomachean Ethics* iii.1.1110a22–24.
8. *Nicomachean Ethics* iii.1.1110a32–4.
9. Aristotle also makes a confusing distinction between an "involuntary agent" and a "not voluntary" agent. For one way of resolving Aristotle's puzzling statements see J. O. Urmson (1988), pp. 45–46.
10. *Nicomachean Ethics* iii.5.1113b22–35, 1114a1–3.
11. Ross (1945), p. 198.
12. See Nagel (1982); Williams (1981).
13. Anscombe (1976), p. 9.
14. Irwin (1980), pp. 117–56.
15. Nussbaum (1986), pp. 282–87.
16. Ibid., p. 285.

17. *Nicomachean Ethics* iii.5.1114a3–11.
18. Glover (1970), Ch. 1.
19. Mackie (1987), pp. 203–15.
20. Ibid., p. 204.
21. Mackie (1987), pp. 211–12.
22. Mackie (1987), p. 212.
23. Insanity Defense Work Group (1983), p. 685.

Chapter 3

1. McElroy et al. (1989), p. 358.
2. Emmanuel et al. (1991), p. 950.
3. Krafft-Ebing (1926), pp. 255–58.
4. Ginsberg (1985), p. 1100.
5. Berlin (1989), p. 233.
6. Ibid., p. 258.
7. Ibid., p. 500.
8. Krafft-Ebing (1926), p. 503.
9. Glover (1970), p. 99.
10. Ibid.
11. Glover (1970), p. 98.
12. Mele (1987), p. 23.
13. Feinberg, (1970), p. 282.
14. Gelder et al. (1983), pp. 479–81; MacDonald (1973), p. 48.
15. Feinberg (1970), p. 284.
16. Ibid., p. 287.
17. Ibid., p. 289.
18. It is also interesting to speculate on the role that seemingly inscrutable, incoherent desires play in a person's unconscious mental economy. Freud writes on the connection between Dostoyevsky's pathological gambling and his creative genius:

> He never rested until he had lost everything. For him gambling was a method of self-punishment as well. Time after time he gave his young wife his promise or his word of honour not to play any more or not to play any more on that particular day; and, as she says, he almost always broke it. When his losses had reduced himself and her to the direst need, he derived a second pathological satisfaction from that. He could then scold and humiliate himself before her, invite her to despise him and to feel sorry that she had married such an old sinner; and when he had thus unburdened his conscience, the whole business would begin again next day. His young wife accustomed herself to this cycle, for she had noticed that the one thing that offered any real hope of salvation — his literary production — never went better than when they had lost everything and pawned their last possessions. (Freud 1973, p. 191)

19. Feinberg (1970), p. 298.
20. Brodeur (1985), p. 600.
21. McCall (1985), p. 594. There is a minor problem with formulations like this, but one that is worth mentioning. In duress, an agent acts contrary to his desires. But if he acts, is it not necessary that he have at least some sort of desire to act? In other words, if a person acts intentionally, then it seems that this action must have been caused by a desire to act, even if it is only a desire to avoid harm. McCall tries to get around this difficulty by arguing against a causal theory of action, but the problem does not warrant these lengths. In duress, it is not necessary that the agent choose to act *contrary* to his desires; it is only necessary that the action that the agent chooses have consequences that are strongly undesirable. For a plea of duress we do not require that an agent has acted in *complete* opposition to his desires — only that he has a strong desire not to act.
22. In a legal context, the term "duress" is generally employed when the source of the duress is another person, while "necessity" is used when the source is natural forces. Although in the case of psychiatric disorders necessity is probably a more appropriate term, for clarity's sake I have chosen to use duress, because the term necessity mistakenly implies that the necessitated action was compelled.
23. Baker (1985), p. 605.
24. On this, see Richards (1987), pp. 21–36.
25. Winer and Pollock (1985), p. 1817.
26. Winer and Pollock (1985), p. 1817; Goodman and Guze (1989), pp. 125–47.
27. See, for example, Bond and Hutchison (1960), pp. 23–25; Emmanuel et al (1991), p. 950; Gelder et al. (1983), pp. 479–81; MacDonald (1973), p. 48; Lester (1975), p. 8.
28. Gombay (1985), pp. 579–81.
29. Brodeur (1985), p. 600.
30. See, for example, Allen (1969), p. 466–67.
31. Bond and Hutchison (1965), pp. 246–50.
32. Ibid., p. 247.
33. Ibid.
34. For a discussion of necrophilia and related crimes, see Rosman and Resnick (1989).

Chapter 4

1. Tyrer, Casey, and Ferguson (1991), p. 463.
2. *The ICD–10 Classification of Mental and Behavioral Disorders*, p. 200.
3. Ibid., p. 202.
4. DSM–IV, p. 630.
5. Frances (1986), p. 173; Kernberg (1984), pp. 77–78.
6. See Szasz (1961).
7. Wootton (1959), p. 250.

8. However, diagnoses of some organic diseases are usually made solely on the basis of behavior, such as Alzheimer's disease.

9. Cummins (1980), p. 211.

10. Ibid.

11. Ibid., p. 212.

12. Ibid.

13. Fields (1987), p. 201–5.

14. Ibid., p. 204.

15. Ibid.

16. Cummins (1980), p. 212.

17. Tyrer et al. (1991), p. 463.

18. An exception, in some cases, might be the psychopathic personality, which is discussed in chapter 5.

Chapter 5

1. I am using the term "psychopath" in a very loose sense. The problems of psychiatric nomenclature will become evident as this chapter progresses.

2. Whitlock (1987), p. 653.

3. Goodwin and Guze (1989), p. 241.

4. Ibid.

5. Jaspers (1923), p. 441.

6. Gelder et al. (1983), pp. 479–81; Kolb and Brodie (1982), p. 608; Goodwin and Guze (1989), pp. 240–54. Most of my discussion in this chapter will concern the sort of psychopath who is most often discussed in the North American psychiatric literature — occasionally called the "primary psychopath" — rather than the sort of psychopath discussed in the British and Australasian literature. Probably the foremost writers on psychopathy in North America are Cleckley and R. D. Hare (see, for example, Hare and Schalling 1978, and Hare 1983).

7. Cleckley (1976), p. 364.

8. Gelder et al. (1983), p. 114.

9. Cleckley (1976), p. 346.

10. Howard (1986), p. 796; Blackburn (1988), p. 509. Unless otherwise noted, the arguments in this chapter refer to the primary psychopath.

11. See Arrington (1979); Murphy (1972); Haksar (1964 and 1965); Duff (1977); Smith (1984–5); Holmes (1991).

12. For a brief but helpful discussion of the difficulties of interpreting what "understanding the difference between right and wrong" means for delusional patients, see Goldstein (1989).

13. Even those people in moral disagreement with the majority, such as civil disobedients, we still generally want to hold morally responsible for their actions. We may think that these actions are *praiseworthy,* of course, rather than blameworthy, but this still entails accountability.

14. We have reason to believe that Aristotle, to whom the original formulation of ignorance as an excusing condition is attributed, would not have counted the ignorance of the psychopath as the sort of ignorance which excuses. Aristotle says that it is not ignorance of "the universal" which excuses but rather ignorance of "particulars" — "the circumstances of the action and the objects with which it is concerned" (*Nicomachean Ethics* iii.1.1110a32–4).

15. Cleckley (1976), p. 209.

16. Ibid. p. 214.

17. Ibid, p. 149.

18. Ryle (1967), p. 74.

19. Ibid, p. 73.

20. See Howard (1986). What follows is a simplified summary of only part of Howard's results, much of which dealt with another experimental paradigm and also with secondary psychopaths.

21. For more speculation and an extended discussion on this question, see Elliott and Gillett (1992).

22. Wittgenstern (1958), p. 223.

23. Duff (1977), p. 194.

24. Robins et al (1991), pp. 258–90.

25. The Quality Assurance Project (1991), p. 545.

Chapter 6

1. This case is adapted from De Pauw, Karel and T. Krystyna Szulecka (1988), pp. 91–96.

2. For a detailed and eloquent argument for the indispensability of these sorts of feelings for morality, see Bernard Williams's essay "Moral Luck," in Williams (1984).

3. See DSM–IV (1994).

4. Goldstein (1989), p. 62.

5. Goldstein (1989), p. 62.

6. For an excellent fictional description of the paranoid personality disorder and its violent results, see Pete Dexter's novel, *Paris Trout.*

7. Rogers et al. (1988), p. 251.

8. Adapted from a case described by De Pauw, Karel and T. Krystyna Szulecka (1988), pp. 91–96.

9. For an interesting consideration of similar issues, see Dennett (1978), pp. 150–53.

10. Kleinig (1985), p. 75.

11. Although in general, excuses are value-neutral and justifications value-dependent, the distinction between the two can easily blur. Glover (1970, pp. 175–78) cites the case of Adolf Eichmann, who sent countless Jews to their deaths in World War II concentration camps. Eichmann later claimed that he was unaware of the fate of these Jews, and moreover, that he was merely following orders from a higher author-

ity. Ignore for a moment the factual implausibility of Eichmann's claims. First, he is claiming ignorance of the consequences of his actions. Ignorance is an excuse, and normally we would regard someone as excused from responsibility on these grounds unless he was negligently ignorant. Eichmann may well be seen as negligently ignorant in this case, because we usually expect that a person take care to inform himself of the possible consequences of his actions, especially when the possible harm of these consequences is very great. However, Eichmann has a second claim — that he was following orders. He might also claim that his duty is to follow orders blindly, without examining their moral acceptability or their possible harmful consequences. This second claim, that of following orders, is not an appeal to be excused, but rather a claim that his action was justified. Here is where the line between justification and excuse becomes fuzzy: Eichmann is claiming that he is justified in keeping himself ignorant, and that ignorance is a valid excuse. So what we must decide in this case is not whether ignorance is a valid excuse, but rather whether Eichmann was *justified* in intentionally keeping himself ignorant of the consequences of his actions. (For a good discussion of Glover's treatment of the Eichmann case, see Cooper 1987, pp. 89–95.)

12. This case is adapted from Ratner (1981), pp. 23–32.

13. Ratner (1981), p. 31.

14. Ratner (1981), pp. 30–31.

15. For a good discussion of how mood can affect the appreciation of wrongfulness, see Goldstein (1989b).

16. Adapted from Meyers (1987), pp. 373–416.

17. Ibid., p. 383.

18. Ibid., p. 384.

Chapter 7

1. Cited in McCall (1975), pp. 188–90.

2. Culver and Gert (1982), pp. 20–63.

3. Ibid.

4. Michael Moore points to this condition among several others, in Moore (1984), p. 105.

5. Hume (1878), p. 196.

6. Ibid., p. 197.

7. Moore (1984), p. 102.

8. Moore argues that the law presumes that desires can be incorrect, in Moore (1984), pp. 103–4.

9. Goldstein (1989b), p. 124.

10. For one version of the argument that certain ends of action are irrational, see Culver and Gert, pp. 26–35.

11. Reid (1850), p. 342.

12. Reid (1850), p. 333.

13. Ibid., p. 342.

14. Ibid.

15. Henderson and Gillespie (1969), p. 279.

16. Meyers (1987), p. 389.

17. President's Commission for the Study of Ethical Problems in Medicine and Biomedical and Behavioral Research, *Making Health Care Decisions,* Vol. 1 (1982), pp. 57–60.

Bibliography

Abrams, Natalie. 1979. "Definitions of Mental Illness and the Insanity Defense." *Journal of Psychiatry and Law* Winter, 443–60.

Adams, Robert. 1985. "Involuntary Sins." *The Philosophical Review* XCIV:1, 3–31.

Allen, Clifford. 1969. *A Textbook of Pychosexual Disorders.* London: Oxford University Press.

Anscombe, G. E. M. 1976. *Intention.* Ithaca: Cornell University Press.

Aristotle. 1987. *Nicomachean Ethics.* Trans. Ross, David. Oxford: Oxford University Press.

Arrington, Robert. 1979. "Practical Reason, Responsibility and the Psychopath." *Journal for the Theory of Social Behavior* 9, 71–80.

Baker, Brenda. 1985. "Duress, Responsibility and Deterrence." *Dialogue* 24, 605–12.

Barnes, Jonathan, Malcolm Schofield, and Richard Sorabji. 1977. *Articles on Aristotle, Volume 2: Ethics and Politics.* London: Duckworth.

Beauchamp, Tom L., and James F. Childress. 1994. *Principles of Biomedical Ethics,* 4ᵗʰ ed. New York: Oxford University Press.

Berlin, Fred. 1989. "The Paraphilias and Depo-Provera: Some Medical, Ethical and Legal Considerations." *Bulletin of the American Academy of Psychiatry and the Law* 17:3, 233–39.

Blackburn, R. 1988. "On Moral Judgements and Personality Disorders." *British Journal of Psychiatry* 153, 505–12.

Bond, I. K., and H. C. Hutchison. 1960. "Application of Reciprocal Inhibition Therapy to Exhibitionism." *The Canadian Medical Association Journal* 83.

Bradley, F. H. 1927. *Ethical Studies.* Oxford: Clarendon Press.

Brand, Myles. 1984. *Intending and Acting: Toward a Naturalized Action Theory.* Cambridge: MIT Press.

Brodeur, Jean Paul. 1985. "Compelled To Choose." *Dialogue* 24, 597–603.

Cleckley, Hervey. 1976. *The Mask of Sanity.* St. Louis: C. V. Mosby.

Cooper, Neil. 1987. "On Evading Responsibility." *Journal of Applied Philosophy* 4, 89–94.

133

Cooper, A. M., A. J. Frances, and M. H. Sacks. 1986. *The Personality Disorders and Neuroses.* New York: Basic Books.

Culver, Charles, and Bernard Gert. 1982. *Philosophy in Medicine.* New York: Oxford University Press.

Cummins, Robert. 1980. "Culpability and Mental Disorder." *Canadian Journal of Philosophy* 10, 207–32.

Davidson, Donald. 1973. "Freedom to Act." In Honderich, Ted, ed., *Essays on Freedom of Action.* London: Routledge and Kegan Paul.

De Pauw, Karel W., and T. Krystyna Szulecka. 1988. "Dangerous Delusions: Violence and the Misidentification Syndromes." *British Journal of Psychiatry* 152, 91–96.

Dennett, Daniel. 1973. "Mechanism and Responsibility." In Honderich, Ted, ed., *Essays on Freedom of Action.* London: Routledge and Kegan Paul.

Dennett, Daniel. 1978. *Brainstorms: Philosophical Essays on Mind and Psychology.* Montgomery, Vt.: Bradford Books.

Diagnostic and Statistical Manual of Mental Disorders: DSM–IV, 1994. Washington, D.C.: American Psychiatric Association.

Downie, R. S. 1967. "Forgiveness." *Philosophical Quarterly* 15:59.

Downie, R. S., and Elizabeth Telfer. 1980. *Caring and Curing: A Philosophy of Medicine and Social Work.* London: Methuen.

Downie, R. S., and K. C. Calman. 1987. *Healthy Respect: Ethics in Health Care.* London: Faber and Faber.

Duff, Anthony. 1977. "Psychopathy and Moral Understanding." *American Philosophical Quarterly* 14, 189–200.

Edel, Abraham. 1982. *Aristotle and his Philosophy.* Chapel Hill: University of North Carolina Press.

Elliott, Carl. 1991a. "The Rules of Insanity: Commentary on Psychopathic Disorder: A Category Mistake?" *Journal of Medical Ethics* 17:2, 79–85.

Elliott, Carl, and Britt Elliott. 1991b. "From the Patient's Point of View: Medical Ethics and the Moral Imagination." *Journal of Medical Ethics* 17:4, 173–78.

Elliott, Carl. 1991c. "Competence as Accountability." *Journal of Clinical Ethics* (Fall) 2:3.

Elliott, Carl. 1991d. "On Psychiatry and Souls: Walker Percy and the Ontological Lapsometer." *Perspectives in Biology and Medicine* 2, 236–48.

Elliott, Carl. 1992a. "Constraints and Heroes." *Bioethics* 6:1, 1–11.

Elliott, Carl, and Grant Gillett. 1992b. "Moral Insanity and Practical Reason." *Philosophical Psychology* 5:1, 53–67.

Elliott, Carl. 1992c. "Where Ethics Comes From and What to Do About It." *The Hastings Center Report* 22:4, 28–35.

Elliott, Carl. 1992d. "Everything Is What It Is." *Inquiry* 34, 525–38.

Emmanuel, Naresh P., R. Bruce Lydiard, and James C. Ballenger. 1991. "Fluoxetine Treatment of Voyeurism" (letter). *American Journal of Psychiatry* 148:7, 950.

Feinberg, Joel. 1970. *Doing and Deserving.* Princeton: Princeton University Press.

Feinberg, Joel, and Hyman Gross. 1975. *Philosophy of Law.* Belmont, Calif.: Wadsworth Publishing Company.

Fields, L. 1987. "Exoneration of the Mentally Ill." *Journal of Medical Ethics* 13.

Harrington, A. 1972. *Psychopaths*. London: If Books.

Hart, H. L. A. 1968. *Punishment and Responsibility: Essays in the Philosophy of Law*. New York: Oxford University Press.

Hart, H. L. A., and Tony Honore. 1985. *Causation in the Law*, 2ⁿᵈ ed. Oxford: Clarendon Press.

Heath, Peter. 1971. "Trying and Attempting." *Proceedings of the Aristotelian Society* 45, 193–208.

Holmes, Colin. 1991. "Psychopathic Disorder: A Category Mistake?" *Journal of Medical Ethics* 17, 277–85.

Honderich, Ted, ed. 1973. *Essays on Freedom of Action*. London: Routledge and Kegan Paul.

Howard, R. C., George Fenton, and Peter Fenwick. 1984. "The Contingent Negative Variation, Personality and Antisocial Behavior." *British Journal of Psychiatry* 144, 463–74.

Howard, R. C. 1986. "Psychopathy: A Psychobiological Perspective." *Personality and Individual Differences* 7, 795–806.

Hughes, Graham. 1975. "Attempting the Impossible." In Feinberg, Joel, and Hyman Gross, *Philosophy of Law*. Belmont, Calif.: Wadsworth Publishing Company.

Hume, David. 1878 (originally 1739). *A Treatise of Human Nature*, Vol. 2. London: Longmans, Green and Co.

ICD–10 Classification of Mental and Behavioral Disorders. 1992. Geneva: World Health Organization.

Insanity Defense Work Group. 1983. "American Psychiatric Association Position Statement on the Insanity Defense." *American Journal of Psychiatry* 140:6, 681–88.

Irwin, T. H. 1980. "Reason and Responsibility in Aristotle." In Rorty, Amelie, *Essays on Aristotle's Ethics*. Berkeley: Berkeley University Press.

Jaspers, Karl. 1923. *General Psychopathology*. Manchester: Manchester University Press.

Kaplan, H. I., A. M. Freedman, and B. J. Sadock. 1985. *Comprehensive Textbook of Psychiatry*. Baltimore: Williams and Wilkins.

Kenner, Lionel. 1967. "On Blaming." *Mind* 76, 238–49.

Kenny, Anthony. 1978. *Free Will and Responsibility*. London: Routledge and Kegan Paul.

Kenny, Anthony. 1985. *The Ivory Tower: Essays in Philosophy and Public Policy*. New York: Basil Blackwell.

Kernberg, Otto. 1984. *Severe Personality Disorders*. New Haven: Yale University Press.

Kleinig, John. 1985. *Ethical Issues in Psychosurgery*. London: George Allen and Unwin.

Kolb, Lawrence, and Keith Brodie. 1982. *Modern Clinical Psychiatry*, 10ᵗʰ ed. Philadelphia: Saunders.

Krafft-Ebing, R. V. 1926. *Psychopathia Sexualis*. New York: Physicians and Surgeons Book Company.

Lester, David. 1975. *Unusual Sexual Behavior: The Standard Deviations.* Springfield, Ill.: Charles C. Thomas Publishers.

Levi, Don. 1989. "What's Luck Got to Do With It?." *Philosophical Investigations* 12, 1–13.

Mackie, J. L. 1987. *Ethics: Inventing Right and Wrong.* London: Penguin.

Malcolm, Janet. 1982. *Psychoanalysis: The Impossible Profession.* New York: Vantage Books.

MacDonald, John M. 1973. *Indecent Exposure.* Springfield, Ill.: Charles C. Thomas Publishers.

McCormick, Suzanne, and Irving Thalberg. 1967. "Trying." *Dialogue* 6, 29–46.

McElroy, Susan L., Paul E. Keck, Harrison G. Pope, and James I. Hudson. 1989. "Pharmacological Treatment of Kleptomania and Bulimia Nervosa." *Journal of Clinical Pharmacology* 9:5, 358–60.

Mele, Alfred. 1987. *Irrationality.* Oxford: Oxford University Press.

Mele, Alfred. 1987. "Intentional Action and Wayward Causal Chains: The Problem of Tertiary Waywardness." *Philosophical Studies* 51, 55–60.

Meyers, C. J. 1987. "A Visitor from Another Planet: The Case of D. J." *The Journal of Psychiatry and Law* 15:3, 373–416.

Moore, Michael. 1984. *Law and Psychiatry: Rethinking the Relationship.* Cambridge: Cambridge University Press.

Morris, Norval. 1982. *Madness and the Criminal Law.* Chicago: University of Chicago Press.

Murphy, Jeffrey G. 1972. "Moral Death: A Kantian Essay on Psychopathy." *Ethics* 82, 284–98.

Nagel, Thomas. 1982. "Moral Luck." In Watson, Gary, *Free Will.* Oxford: Oxford University Press.

Nussbaum, Martha. 1986. *The Fragility of Goodness: Luck and Ethics in Greek Tragedy and Philosophy.* Cambridge: Cambridge University Press.

Peacocke, Arthur, and Grant Gillett, eds. 1987. *Persons and Personality.* Oxford: Basil Blackwell.

Perry, John, ed. 1975. *Personal Identity.* Berkeley: University of California Press.

President's Commission for the Study of Ethical Problems in Medicine and Biomedical and Behavioral Research. 1982. *Making Health Care Decisions,* Vol. 1. U.S. Government Printing Office.

Quality Assurance Project. 1991. "Treatment Outlines for Antisocial Personality Disorder." *Australian and New Zealand Journal of Psychiatry* 25, 541–47.

Ratner, Richard A. 1981. "Mania, Crime and the Insanity Defense: A Case Report." *Bulletin of the American Academy of Psychiatry and the Law* 9:1.

Rhees, Rush. 1965. "Wittgenstein's Lecture on Ethics: Some Developments in Wittgenstein's View of Ethics." *Philosophical Review* 74.

Reid, William, ed. 1978. *The Psychopath: A Comprehensive Study of Antisocial Disorders and Behaviors.* New York: Brunner/Mazel.

Reid, Thomas. 1850 (originally 1785). *Essays on the Intellectual Powers of Man.* Cambridge: John Bartlett.

Report of the Committee on Mentally Abnormal Offenders. 1975. London: Her Majesty's Stationery Office.

Richards, Norvin. 1987. "Acting Under Duress." *Philosophical Quarterly* 37, 21–36.

Robins, L. N., J. Tipp, and T. Przybeck. 1991. "Antisocial Personality." In Robins, L. N., and D. A. Regier, eds., *Psychiatric Disorders in America.* New York: The Free Press, 258–90.

Rogers, Richard, David Nussbaum, and Roy Gillis. 1988. "Command Hallucinations and Criminality: A Clinical Quandary." *Bulletin of the American Academy of Psychiatry and the Law* 16:3, 251–58.

Rorty, Amelie, ed. 1974. *The Identity of Persons.* Berkeley: University of California Press.

Rorty, Amelie, ed. 1980. *Essays on Aristotle's Ethics.* Berkeley: Berkeley University Press.

Rosman, Jonathan, and Philip Resnick. 1989. "Sexual Attraction to Corpses: Psychiatric Review of Necrophilia." *Bulletin of the American Academy of Psychiatry and the Law* 17:2, 153–62.

Ross, David. 1945. *Aristotle.* London: Methuen and Co.

Ryle, Gilbert. 1967. "On Forgetting the Difference Between Right and Wrong." In Walsh, J. J., and H. L. Shapiro. *Aristotle's Ethics.* Belmont, Calif.: Wadsworth Publishing Company, 70–79.

Ryle, Gilbert. 1949. *Concept of Mind.* London: Hutchinson's University Library.

Schatzki, Theodore. 1983. "The Prescription is Description: Wittgenstein's View of the Human Sciences." In Mitchell, Sollace, and Michael Rosen, eds., *The Need for Interpretation: Contemporary Conceptions of the Philosopher's Task.* New Jersey: Humanities Press.

Silva, J. A., G. B. Leong, R. Weinstock, and C. L. Boyer. 1989. "Capgras Syndrome and Dangerousness." *Bulletin of the American Academy of Psychiatry and Law* 17:1, 5–14.

Singer, Peter. 1986. "All Animals Are Equal." In Singer, Peter, ed., *Applied Ethics.* New York: Oxford University Press.

Smith, Robert J. 1984. "The Psychopath as Moral Agent." *Philosophy and Phenomenological Research* 45, 177–94.

Smith, Adam. 1982. *The Theory of Moral Sentiments.* Indianapolis: Liberty Press.

Strawson, Peter. 1974. *Freedom and Resentment and Other Essays.* London: Methuen.

Sverdlik, Steven. 1988. "Crime and Moral Luck." *American Philosophical Quarterly* 25, 79–86.

Szasz, Thomas. 1961 (1974). *The Myth of Mental Illness: Foundations of a Theory of Personal Conduct,* rev. ed. New York: Harper and Row.

Szasz, Thomas. 1991. "The Religion Called 'Psychiatry.'" In Browning, D. S., and I. S. Evison, eds., *Does Psychiatry Need a Public Policy?* Chicago: Nelson-Hall Publishers.

Tyrer, P., P. Casey, and B. Ferguson. 1991. "Personality Disorder in Perspective." *British Journal of Psychiatry* 159: 463–71.

Urmson, J. O. 1988. *Aristotle's Ethics.* Oxford: Basil Blackwell Ltd.

Walsh, J. J., and H. L. Shapiro. 1967. *Aristotle's Ethics.* Belmont, Calif.: Wadsworth Publishing Company.

Watson, Gary, ed. 1982. *Free Will.* Oxford: Oxford University Press.

Wertheimer, Alan. 1987. *Coercion.* Princeton: Princeton University Press.

West, Donald J., and Alexander Walk, eds. 1977. *Daniel McNaughton: His Trial and the Aftermath.* Ashford, Kent: Gaskell Books.

Whitlock, F. A. 1987. "Psychopathic Personality." In Gregory, Richard, ed., *The Oxford Companion to the Mind,* 651–53.

Williams, Bernard. 1973. *Problems of the Self.* Cambridge: Cambridge University Press.

Williams, Bernard. 1981. *Moral Luck: Philosophical Papers 1973–80.* New York: Cambridge University Press.

Winch, Peter. 1971. "Trying and Attempting." *Proceedings of the Aristotelian Society* 45, 209–27.

Winer, J. A., and G. H. Pollock. 1985. "Adjustment and Impulse Control Disorders." In Kaplan, H. I., A. M. Freedman, and B. J. Sadock, eds., *Comprehensive Textbook of Psychiatry III.* Baltimore: Williams and Wilkins.

Winokur, G., and R. Crowe. 1975. "Personality Disorders." In Freedman, A., H. Kaplan, and B. Sadock, eds., *Comprehensive Textbook of Psychiatry II.* Baltimore: Williams and Wilkins.

Wittgenstein, Ludwig. 1958. *Philosophical Investigations.* Trans. Anscombe, G. E. M. New York: Macmillan.

Wootton, Barbara. 1959. *Social Science and Social Pathology.* London: Allen and Unwin.

Zilboorg, Gregory. 1943. *Mind, Medicine and Man.* New York: Harcourt, Brace.

Cases Cited

Durham v. United States, 214 F.2d at 847–75 (D.C. Cir. 1954).

Parsons v. State, 81 Ala. 577, 597, 2 So. 854, (1887).

Regina v. M'Naghten, 10 Clark and F. 200, 8 Eng. Rep. 718 (1843).

State v. Pike, 49 N.H, at 442 (1869).

Index

141